**ALBA HOUSE**
a division of
St. Paul Publications
**Staten Island, N.Y.**

# HEALTH OF

# MIND

# & SOUL

Ignace
Lepp

Originally published under the title. *Hygiene de Came,*
Aubier-Montaigne, Paris, France

Nihil Obstat:
Gall Higgins, O.F.M.Cap.
Censor Librorum

Imprimatur:
✠ Terence J. Cooke, D.D., V.G.

New York, N.Y. — June 30, 1966

Library of Congress Card Number: 66-19717

*"Our civilization is one big body without a soul."*
— *Bergson*

# CONTENTS

# INTRODUCTION

## the sick soul

That the soul, as well as the body, can be sick, seems to be a fact attested to by humanity as far back as humanity was conscious of its specifically human existence. It is unimportant to note that the majority of such sickness in primitive and ancient civilizations was attributed to possession by demons or natural causes. What is more noteworthy is the fact that from the very first there has been a history of efforts to cure sickness in a soul. Between the exorcisms of those early days and the "scientific" psychotherapy of our own days, there is perhaps less real difference than we might like to admit.

These sicknesses of soul have a somewhat more conventional name today; we call them *neuroses* and *psychoses*. Both are susceptible to treatment and cure by a variety of psychotherapeutic processes, neuroses more so than psychoses. For half a century now, thanks to the brilliant discoveries of Dr. Sigmund Freud, psychotherapy has been making immense progress, at least as important as the progress realized in the field of germs and germ-induced bodily sickness since Pasteur. In addition to the psychoanalysis of Freud, properly so-called, the analytic psychoanalysis of Carl Jung, and the individual psychology of Alfred Adler, there are a number of other methods, analytic or synthetic in their orientation, which all have a number of cures to their credit. There is no counting the number of men who, thanks to some form of psychotherapy, have rediscovered their taste for life, happiness in their marriage, a more normal relationship with their parents or children, a better adaptation to the world of reality.

And yet, we need only look carefully at those about us or those whom we happen to meet and we are forced to admit that the progress of psychotherapy has not managed to do away with every trace of neurosis, but only to control its outward expression. Evidence of neurosis is actually more and more widespread. Everything points to the conclusion that our modern-day city living, with the frantic and unnatural rhythm of life it forces upon us, is particularly apt to give rise to neurosis. And thus, the unquestioned effectiveness of the potential cures for neurosis is not so heartening as it ought to be. Before he has recourse to psychotherapy, a person will generally have to go through a good deal of suffering and encounter some very painful opposition in his family, professional, and social life. Besides this, despite all the goodwill in the world, psychotherapy is available to only a small fraction of those who need it. Competent practitioners are far too few to meet the growing need. But a mere increase in the number of competently trained doctors would not, in itself, resolve the problem. Successful psychoanalysis generally has to extend over some months, frequently over several years. As a result, only those who have sufficient time and resources are able to profit from such treatment. Does this mean that everyone else must learn to be resigned to the prospect of life-long neurosis? This is hardly an answer; the solution lies along the road of preventive care.

In the domain of physical health, it is almost universally admitted today that the most effective measure against sickness is preventive medicine. Bodily hygiene, in all its various forms, is being practiced more and more in even the lowest levels of society, even if it consists in nothing more than soap and toothbrush. Indeed, a number of diseases that used to claim thousands of lives every year have now almost completely disappeared, while others have become more manageable or rarer in occurrence; the credit for all this progress goes to preventive medicine. Most enlightened people do not wait for a toothache before they visit their dentist for a regular check-up. Expectant mothers make regular trips to the doctor, as insurance against the various dangers that threaten either their own health or the child they are carrying. Health inspections, at school and work, are another important and effective weapon of preventive medicine. It is not too unlikely to suppose that, in the very near future, despite the vigorous protests of some of their number, the majority of doctors will be servants of public health and that their pay will not be in proportion to the number of sick people they cure, but pro-rated according to the number of patients whose health they have managed to preserve.

Unfortunately, we are not so far advanced in the field of psychic illness. Mental hygiene does exist, to be sure, and it is making progress. But its field of activity is still terribly narrow. Not only the general public, but even the majority of professional educators, seem to be in complete ignorance of its existence; at least they often act as if they had never heard the word "mental hygiene".

This little book hopes to clarify a few points and offer a few practical bits of advice which might be useful especially to parents and educators. Mental hygiene, however, is not just something for children. Each and every one of us needs mental hygiene, for no one is completely immune to mental sickness. If it is true, as the majority of psychotherapists seem to think, that almost all neuroses have their origin in infancy or adolescence, it is also true that they can begin to show their presence at any age. Frequently enough, it takes only a very small thing to keep a disease from rising to the surface, even though it is the source of no little disturbance in the inner consciousness of the subject and creates serious difficulty for his companions and the society in which he lives, and its cure, after a certain age, is more and more difficult.

Mental hygiene obviously has much in common with education, especially when it is a question of mental hygiene for the child. But this little volume is no mere treatise on education. In education, properly so-called, there are a great many aspects which have no relationship whatsoever with the avoidance of psychic conflict and neurosis. But mental hygiene is taken up exclusively with these subjects. We have already explained our theories about psychic illness and its cure in a recent work, *The Depths of the Soul.** Thus there is no need to weigh down the present volume with theoretical considerations. It is enough to recall that:

1. The whole of our psychic activity is at once *conscious* and *unconscious*. The unconscious can disturb the conscious more or less seriously, without the conscious mind always being aware of this disturbance.

2. A certain degree of conflict between the various tendencies of the conscious and unconscious mind in the human psyche is not only of frequent occurrence, but might even be described as normal and even desirable. This conflict is the basis for that dialectic of existence without which there could be neither maturity nor progress in the personality.

3. When, as a result of failure, inhibitions, or other external or internal factors, the ego is no longer in a position to resolve these psychic conflicts which might be considered as normal, the conflicts then threaten to degenerate into *neurosis*. Neurosis is recognizable by a *fear* or an *anxiety* which are out of all

_____

Alba House, 1966.

proportion to their real causes, (or apparently without any cause at all), by a lack of any taste for living, by repeated failure in practically everything that is undertaken, by an inability to adapt to the real conditions of living. The causes of neurosis frequently go back to childhood, sometimes to adolescence, even when the sickness is not visible, as is generally the case, until much later, as a result of new shocks upon the system. These new problems are sometimes quite without any objective seriousness, but the personality threatened by a latent neurosis is too weak to resist them with any real effort.

4. Only *psychotherapy*, such as we have known it for the last half century, is equal to the task of really curing a neurosis. Contrary to the primitive approaches of days gone by, and even the present techniques of certain psychiatrists, psychotherapy is aimed not at the symptoms, which are always more or less superficial, but at the cause and ultimate root of the sickness. There are a wide variety of modern theories and techniques in psychotherapy, but all of them are greatly indebted to the insights and discoveries of Dr. Freud and his first disciples, Jung and Adler, who became the founders of rival schools.

5. I have given my own method the name of *psychosynthesis*, in an effort to show that, contrary to the leanings of orthodox psychoanalysis, I am interested not only in the unconcious, but am at least equally concerned with the conscious self. In all its essential elements, my work is inspired by the writings of Professor C. Jung — his theories seem to me to get deeper into the psychological problems of mental sickness than do those of the other masters.

# PART I

# MENTAL HYGIENE IN THE INFANT

# 1 existence in the womb

Hardly half a century has passed since the days when psychologists and teachers were definitely convinced that experiences going back before the "use of reason" (which was set at seven years of age) had no influence whatsoever on the development of the *moral personality* of a man. Our memory can preserve only a few scattered remnants from this first of our life, and it was generally understood among psychologists that only conscious facts could enter into the make-up of a personality. Thus, there was no need to be concerned with the joys and sorrows of the young child: it was enough to take suitable care of his physical well-being, teaching him to "mind," much as one might teach a puppy or a kitten.

## I. The Freudian Revolution

The psychoanalytic discoveries of Freud represent a veritable revolution in the field of child psychology, and thus in the fundamental principles of education. All the old ideas about childhood and infancy were profoundly shaken. It is now generally accepted that the conscious mind is far from being the whole, or even the predominant part of the human psyche. It is only a very small islet, emerging from the dark and mysterious ocean of the unconscious. Over the course of many years, thanks to living, reflection, culture, and activity, this tiny islet grows bigger and turns into a real continent. But still, it never does (nor could it ever) become coextensive with psychic totality. The unconscious always remains the fountainhead from which the conscious self draws its sustenance, and at the same time it is an abyss which threatens to engulf the conscious self. It follows thus, that everything that is gradually filed away into the unconscious is of supreme importance for our concrete day-to-day existence.

Many psychologists, more or less orthodox disciples of Dr. Freud, take a position which is diametrically opposed to the views of days gone by. They feel that the first years of existence play an almost exclusive role in the structure of a person's psyche. According to these theorists, whatever a man will eventually be, in terms of his psychological life, he already is at the end of these very first years of his life. Did not Freud himself claim that almost all neurotic phenomena are caused by the psychic conflicts of early childhood? And thus, these psychologists feel they are authorized to conclude, based on the observations made by their master, that the sum total of life and psychic activities are determined by the experiences of early childhood.

The psychologist who is not dogmatically Freudian will admit that it is not impossible, *a priori*, for the experiences and impressions of the earliest years to leave a much deeper mark on the unconscious than those of later years. Conscious activity, since it has not yet awakened in the individual, cannot impose its own norms and principles on the psychic activity of the child. For, if it is true that the unconscious acts upon the conscious, it is no less certain that the conscious, in its turn, influences the unconscious.

Still, we cannot follow those of Freud's disciples who seem to consider the unconscious mind of a small child as a sort of *tabula rosa*, or empty vessel, which will be filled only by the personal experiences of the child. The child is, as a matter of fact, the depositary of a vast ancestral heritage from the whole human race, a concept which Jung expresses in the well-chosen term *collective unconscious*. Neither the individual himself nor those who contribute in any capacity to his formation can have any great influence on this collective unconscious, and yet this collective unconscious has an immense role to play in molding our destiny. This means that neither psychology nor education is all-powerful; it certainly does not mean that they are powerless.

## II. Psychic Life Begins in the Womb

Since the collective unconscious is, by definition, outside its realm, mental hygiene, based on depth psychology, looks to the formation of the individual unconscious. Whatever the actual influence of the individual's psychological heritage, it does not, as far as can be determined, establish a real individual determinism in areas which concern the personal happiness or misery of existence.

It does appear to be scientifically established that the individual unconscious begins its development even before birth. Just as the body of the child grows progressively in the mother's womb, the psyche or soul also enjoys a uterine existence of its own. This existence prepares and partially determines, if not the complete psychic life of the individual, at least the guiding lines along which his development will follow once he is born. Whatever the firmness of our convictions on the matter of psychological freedom, we cannot ignore the fact that it is far from absolute. It can be exercised only within a framework whose limits are, in large part, already determined by the period of existence within the womb.

There are a number of scientific works which tend to prove the existence of psychic activity within the womb. But we do not yet know very much about the specific nature of this activity. This we must expect, since the individual does not retain a single conscious memory of these first months of his life, simply because conscious awareness does not begin its development until some time after birth. Psychoanalysts believe that they can assign certain recollections, uncovered in the course of psychoanalysis, to the fetal state of the individual under treatment. Such recollections and memories, granting their existence, could obviously not be visual representations or verbal memories, as is the case for the majority of our conscious memories. They can have come only from the emotions and affective sensation. It is an unquestionable fact that the activity of emotional life precedes the awakening of consciousness.

According to the psychoanalysts, the dreams of some neurotic patients are an expression of this kind of emotion and sensation within the womb. For example, the patient dreams that he is in a dark, damp cave, where he feels perfect security: This dream merely reproduces a memory of sensation from his uterine existence. In keeping with the famous Freudian postulate which claims that a dream is essentially the realization of a frustrated desire, our psychoanalysts interpret such a dream as a feeling of nostalgia, a desire to return to this happy state of secure existence, so different from the real waking life of the patient, where insecurity threatens him from every side. I myself have asked many persons who were struggling with a deep agony of insecurity to draw me a picture, showing themselves in a state of perfect security. It is at least a very curious coincidence that all of them, equivalently, and quite spontaneously, drew pictures that more or less faithfully reproduced the situation of the fetus in his mother's womb. Is it correct to conclude that this is evidence of a real recollection of uterine existence? It is at least probable, but still far from being scientifically proven.

Whatever the nature of the influence which the experiences

of life within the womb later exercise on the psyche, it is beyond question that the emotional states of this period play a significant role in the whole later development of the individual. A number of experiments have been carried on, with chickens and various mammals, and these experiments have definitely established the possibility of psychic trauma in this stage of development. This is also confirmed by observations of the development of the human fetus. But as for concluding, as do certain Freudians, that suicide by drowning, for example, is evidence of the neurotic patient's unconscious desire to return to the uterine state of existence and rediscover the security and freedom from responsibility that he misses in real life — this, in the present state of scientific knowledge on the subject, can be regarded as nothing more than the fruit of a rather active imagination. There are too many neurotic patients who attempt suicide in many other ways beside drowning, and a good many of them have no desire to take their own lives at all.

## III. Insights of Popular Wisdom

Popular intuitive wisdom, obviously drawing on the treasures filed away in the collective unconscious, was well aware of the great significance of life in the womb, long before the discoveries of psychoanalysis. Remember that in ancient Greece, expectant mothers were very carefully kept from any contact with anything ugly or evil. They were taken to see inspiring statues and handsome youths and beautiful maidens, in the firm conviction that such practices would promote the well-being of the unborn child. There was more in question here than mere interest in the physical beauty of the children. Plato, whose philosophy is such an apt expression of the Greek ideal of life, regarded the category of the beautiful as having a meaning that was at one and the same time moral, psychological, and physical.

The old country women, in our own modern society, share this Greek point of view without even being aware of the fact. This alone might be evidence enough of an hereditary intuitive knowledge, common to the whole of the human race. These people take great pains to keep expectant mothers (and even their cattle, when they are about to have their young) from all emotional shock, from anything that might leave a disagreeable impression on them — in order to promote the well-being of the unborn young. I once listened to an old peasant woman, who made no pretense to any intellectual depth or schooling at all, explaining the neurotic tendencies of her grandson as the result of a deep emotional shock experienced by his mother, during her pregnancy, on learning of an accident that had killed his brother. Another old peasant woman was discussing the rather disappointing character of a young lady: "What do you expect? Her mother was terribly frightened by a brawl between two drunks when she was carrying that girl." And we often hear simple country folk advising expectant mothers to "take it easy and not overdo it: think of the child you're carrying."

Popular wisdom and depth psychology are thus agreed on the necessity of applying the rules for mental hygiene, beginning with the child's existence within the womb.

### IV. Preparing the Future Parents

It is neither a whim nor a paradox to say that the psychological formation of the individual has to begin with the psychological formation of his parents. Neurotic tendencies in the parents are a definite threat to the psychic equilibrium of the children. Every psychotherapist knows from experience that the chief obstacle to the cure of young neurotics under their care stems from the neurotic condition of their parents. In order to cure the child, they also have to examine and try to cure the parents — and this is possible in only a very few cases. From the point of view of the child's psychological health, the ideal solution would be for future parents to try to eliminate all neurotic tendencies before marriage. This will make it possible for the child's life (even within the womb) to unfold without too many traumatic shocks.

Still, it is not at all infrequent, even in a family that shows no neurotic tendencies at all, for the first child to suffer from a more or less serious psychic imbalance, while the other children show no traces of such a disorder. According to my own personal observations, this is most frequently the case in young Catholic families, when husband and wife are both virgins and when the first conception takes place shortly after their marriage. It would seem that the explanation for this is to be found in the anxieties occasioned by sexual taboos. These taboos make the beginning of sexual relations an occasion for apprehension rather than pleasure.

It frequently happens that young women, no matter what their education and personal breadth of thinking in other areas, are still influenced, in their unconscious and without being aware of it, by time-honored prejudices of their family and surroundings. Thus they look upon sex more or less implicitly as something really shameful, or at least as a fatal concession that the spirit has to make to the flesh. This dichotomy of flesh-spirit, an idea that is really more Manichean than Christian, has survived in the minds of far too many Christians. It is true, however, that, thanks to the efforts and influence of modern Christian education and such activities as Cana Conferences and retreats, youth clubs and Catholic Action, young Christian men and women have a much more positive attitude towards sex than do their parents. For the present, however, it is only their conscious attitude that has changed. The unconscious, in all too many cases, is still caught up in a thousand false notions and ideas which have somehow managed to survive the demise of Puritanism and Jansenism.

Jean, a doctor of medicine, 27 years old, went to see the psychologist. Married for almost two weeks, she and her husband had not yet consummated their marriage. Every time her husband attempted sexual intimacies with her, there was a sudden contraction of her sexual organs, so painful that neither her husband's most delicate consideration nor her own extreme effort and concentration were able to produce any effect. The gynecologist whom they consulted could only assure them that everything was quite normal on the physical plane.

Jean had belonged to an active youth club for many years and spoke of sexual matters without the least trace of false modesty, with the freedom of expression one expects to find in young medical students. But still every time her husband attempted sexual intimacy with her, she experienced this sudden terrible panic which she could not explain. To their great sorrow, husband and wife were thinking of terminating their marriage; but the psychologist warned them to do nothing rash.

After a few sessions, the psychologist discovered that Jean's parents, although they practiced no formal religion, were still very much puritans in their outlook. Her mother's concern for modesty had become a genuine obsession. As a small girl, Jean was frequently scolded and sometimes even severely punished for what her mother considerd a lack of proper modesty in her conduct. The nuns, who were her teachers from the age of 6 to 17, used to talk constantly about "purity" without being sure that the children had a clear notion of what they meant. It is not at all suprising that, under such conditions, the concept of sex was always associated with ideas of impurity and guilt in Jean's unconscious. Neither her medical studies nor the frank attitudes and ideas of her group of young Catholics had been able to change this association of ideas. A dozen sessions with the psychologist were enough: the young bride was able to accept her husband's sexual intimacies without any anxiety. Her conscious self had managed to integrate these more positive attitudes into her unconscious.

In the majority of other cases of this same kind, the anxiety experienced is not strong enough to make the sexual act completely impossible, and there is thus no reason for going to the psychologist. But still these unconscious feelings of apprehension and anxiety frequently have a most unfortunate influence on the first conception and pregnancy.

Doctor André Berge, one of the best French specialists in child psychology, writes that the child must be conceived in joy, that his birth must not be looked forward to with dread, but positively willed and desired by his parents. These principles need to be very strictly understood. It is not enough, as is frequently the case, for husband and wife to want a child in the hopes that his presence in the home will somehow smooth over the lack of true love between them, or even less, in the hope that he will prolong the family name. Conception cannot really take place in joy unless the child is longed for as the fruit and consecration of their married love.

## V. *Conceived in Joy*

For the conception to take place in joy requires a certain number of practical conditions. We are here presuming the essential condition of mutual love between husband and wife. People of romantic bent like to describe the difference, in the families of the aristocracy or bourgeoisie between children born from "marriages of reason," in which there is no love, and those conceived out of love but outside the legal bonds of matrimony. This distinction over-simplifies the problem; but the idea on which it is based is certainly sound.

Pleasure, obviously, is not the same thing as joy, and pleasure has been known to exist even in the midst of suffering.

Nonetheless, psychologically speaking, in so complex an area as that of sexual love, sense pleasure greatly promotes the development of inner joy.

In the light of the preceding paragraph, the most important factor for assuring that conception will take place in joy, is for the sex act to have lost all its overtones of apprehension and anxiety for husband and wife, particularly for the wife. It is desirable, insofar as possible, for the woman to have arrived at the stage where she can make a generous gift of self and still have a deep appreciation and enjoyment of the organic pleasures involved. But experience has shown that in the vast majority of cases, such a stage is arrived at only after a few months, and sometimes only after a year or two of married life. And the stronger her unconscious inhibitions, the more time the woman will need to arrive at a true sense of pleasure in the physical act.

Insofar as the psychologist's own experience can serve as a guide in such a delicate matter, we believe that it is possible to establish a principle that, except for special cases, conception is not desirable in the very first months of marriage. The problems and difficulties of the material order which the great majority of young married couples have to face in our day already make it difficult enough to face conception and pregnancy with anything like joy. But most of all it is important for the future mother to have the time she needs to arrive at as perfect a sexual development and adjustment as possible. There are, of course, some women who do not arrive at such a state until after one or even two pregnancies: what we are recommending here is not of universal application. But still, for the vast majority of women, a pregnancy which arrives before the experience of real pleasure in orgasm has the effect of concentrating all their emotional attitudes on the mystery of child-bearing and birth. Sexual relations become merely a more or less disagreeable road to the joys of motherhood. Thus they have no immediate joy to look forward to, and as a result some women who, at the outset, were bothered with only slight inhibitions now become definitely frigid. The evil consequences to which such an unhappy condition can easily lead, are too well known to enumerate, both for the personal happiness of the wife and for the success of the marriage.

Many young husbands, particularly in very fervent Christian environments, desire nothing so ardently as the earliest possible conception of their first child. If after two or three months of marriage their wife is not pregnant, they are disturbed; they begin to see themselves as a family condemned to grow old without children.

The psychologist whose business it is to consult with husbands of this kind, generally has no difficulty in discovering that their ardent desire for a child is really quite superficial. It touches only the conscious part of the psyche, whereas the unconscious is riddled with anxiety. On the one hand they would very much like to experiment with the joys and pleasures of sexual love before becoming a father, but on the other hand they feel that they must first realize the "primary purpose" of marriage. It would be regrettable were we to train our young people to believe that the only purpose of marriage is the child. We know in fact and must insist on this, that marriage is also the highest expression of, and the greatest means towards fostering, the mutual love of man and woman. In this connection it is important to insist also on the intrinsic value, beauty, and sacramental status of sexual love. Neither morals nor the birth-rate would suffer from such an orientation.

It is not within the object of this book to advise for or against conception taking place on the honeymoon, or at any time before the husband and wife are emotionally prepared for the event. Each couple must follow an enlightened conscience in this respect. It is enough for the purpose of this little book to call these facts to the attention of all those who, in any capacity whatever, have a contribution to make to family happiness and development. Their first task is to convince the young married people with whom they deal, that procreation is not the only truly noble purpose of sexual union, that sex is not only legitimate in itself but beautiful and noble insofar as it is a symbol and expression of the communion of heart and mind and soul that joins husband and wife together. Paul the Apostle, singing the beauties of this union of love between man and woman, goes so far as to compare it to the union which exists between Christ and his Church and does not even allude to procreation. This should be enough to satisfy even the most scrupulous conscience. Whatever the case may be, putting off the social purpose of marriage, procreation, for one or two months or years in no way violates the intrinsic obligations of the marriage contract or of the sacrament.

In an area composed almost exclusively of special and particular cases, it is all but impossible to set up laws of universal application. Thus the advice given here is only an indication based on cases that we have had the opportunity to observe. A delay of the first pregnancy may, in some cases, be desirable to assure a minimum of material security for the young couple while not denying them the mutual joy of enriching sexual love. On the other hand, it would be well to weigh psychological factors, e.g. — whether the husband or the wife have disturbances in the sexual area reaching a neurotic level.

## VI. Carried in Happiness....

Although scientific studies of the effect of the mother's emotional condition — joy, anxiety, etc. — on the child's happiness are not sufficiently numerous or conclusive to warrant a definitive statement, still there is evidence of a sort which may indicate that the mother's happiness or unhappiness during the prenatal period may not be without its effect at least in many cases. This aspect of the question is the primary object of the popular wisdom to which we referred above, whether it be that of the ancient Greeks, or the simple common people of our own times. The conditions under which conception takes place are beyond its scope: it takes the discoveries of modern psychology to bring out that side of the question.

It is psychologically impossible for a woman to look forward to the birth of her child with any feelings of real happiness unless she knows that she herself is loved and secure. This concept of security must obviously not neglect the material and economic factor, particularly in dealing with our Western civilization, where a minimum of physical well-being and comfort are absolutely indispensable for being happy. When working conditions and particularly living conditions make this necessary feeling of material security difficult or impossible, there will necessarily always be some harmful repercussions, on the psychological plane, for the unborn child. For many young couples, this is a further argument in favor of the advice for putting off the first pregnancy for at least a year and spacing the following pregnancies at suitable intervals.

But infinitely more important, for the expectant mother, is the feeling of moral security. And this feeling is possible only if she can have a complete and total trust in her husband, counting on his love and tenderness. What is more, she needs to know that he is *interested* in the child that is on its way. In theory, such an interest might be taken for granted, but psychologically it is not always so simple. Whereas, the mother quickly becomes physically conscious of the presence of the child beginning to take human form within her womb, the same child will not begin to exist in a really concrete way for the father until after he is born. Only his love for his wife can make him intensely interested in someone who does not yet even exist as far as the father's sense perception is concerned. Most men experience such an interest without any real difficulty, because they really love their wives. This is only an added confirmation of what we have said above, that the only parents who are "worthwhile" for a child are parents who are in love.

## VII. The Trauma of Birth

The normal terminus of existence in the womb is birth. This experience, on the psychological plane, is a veritable revolution for the young person. The passage from the security and passivity of life in the womb into the "light of day" involves him in the deepest emotional upheavals that he will ever have to face in the course of his whole life. Freud sees birth as a particularly serious trauma to which he attributes the feelings of anxiety that plague so many people. Other psychologists find slightly different nuances. According to them, birth is not naturally a trauma, but it *can become* so due to unfavorable conditions. Thus it can become whenever the difficulties or complications of childbirth require the intervention of violent and unnatural procedures, such as Caesarian section, the use of forceps, etc. As a matter of fact, all the patients I have ever dealt with who had been brought into the world through such techniques still carried an easily recognizable stigma from the experience. Such observations, of course, are not enough for any kind of absolute generalization.

Even the "normal" pains of childbirth in the mother, particularly when they are intensified by a feeling of fear or anxiety, can have a traumatic influence on the child.

In being born, the child faces more or less painful contacts with his new environment, the noise that strikes his sense of hearing, the air he has to breathe, the suffocation that constantly seems to threaten him. Everything we express by the more or less flexible term "world" strikes against the unconscious of the newly born child like an army of hostile forces. Our adult consciousness has obviously failed to retain any trace of this emotional upheaval, but its influence on our unconscious mind is still there.

The traumatic effects of birth can be combatted by measures that are almost certain to be effective. The mother's love, expressed in an outgoing tenderness and constant care, is *the* perfect antidote. This is a further argument in favor of the principle that the child must be positively wanted. It is only on this condition that it can be received with the joy and love which are as important as the air it breathes and the nourishment it drinks.

In this respect, it is not good for the expectant parents to be too definite about the sex of the child they are expecting, any more than they are overly concerned about the color of his eyes or hair. The disappointment which could result at not seeing her own or her husband's desires fulfilled in this area could easily be enough to cool the spontaneity of the mother's instinctive love for her newborn child, and the tender unconscious of the child would surely register this shock. Never must the child be made to feel guilty for having been born.

The psychologist can only rejoice at the recent progress in the development of painless childbirth. The new techniques are enough, in many cases, to combat the traumatic effects of birth. The psychological preparation of the expectant mother at the hands of a specialist who is informed on all the aspects of the complex problem of birth, can contribute much to the creation of those conditions of joy and security which we have recognized as being essential to the child's life within the womb. As for the time of childbirth itself, if it can be faced without pain or anxiety, the baby obviously has everything to gain.

# 2 early childhood

The psychology of the baby after birth is obviously much more accessible than that of the child within the womb. We are in a position to observe his behavior and compare it with the reactions of other children of the same age and similar circumstances. What is more, exploration of the unconscious in adult persons uncovers traces and reminiscences which unquestionably go back to the nursing period. The only surprising element in this whole question is the fact that psychologists were so long in developing an interest in the psychology of early childhood. Perhaps there was some unconscious anxiety at play. As the famous psychologist once remarked, only half in jest: "How easy it was to be a parent before psychology came along and complicated everything!"

## I. *Weaning*

According to Freud, it is the pleasure principle that, more than any other consideration, determines the psychological behavior of the individual. Thus, there are three successive stages in the experience of the child: *oral, anal, and genital,* according as he seeks and finds his most intense pleasure in one or another of these areas. We have already spoken of what happens when this point of Freudian psychology is applied too systematically and too summarily.* It goes far beyond the limits of probability when it makes sexual pleasure the prototype of all pleasure.

Still it is an unquestionable fact that the first pleasurable sensations the newborn child experiences come from sucking the nipple of his mother's breast, or as the case might be, the nipple on his baby bottle. A mother whose milk is insufficient to satisfy the appetite of her child might very well be the involuntary cause of a feeling of frustration which he will suffer from in his adult life.

The indispensable process of weaning stands out as a particularly serious traumatic factor. It is not without very good reason that psychotherapists give the name "weaning complex" to a whole nucleus of psychic problems which they frequently encounter in their practice.

It is, of course, true, and we shall have occasion to speak further of it, that more frequently than weaning itself, properly so-called, there are many other separations from the mother, while the child is still at a very tender age, that figure in the make-up of the weaning complex.

Most of the time, the baby bottle will be substituted for the mother's breast, initially or after some few months, without any traumatic effect at all. But for this to be the case, it is most important that at the first moment that this change is made the child is not made to feel frustrated of any of the tenderness which he normally experiences when he is nursed at his mother's breast. When as is generally the case, bottle-feeding follows breast-feeding, it is a good idea for this passage from one method to the other to be made gradually: for a certain period the baby should be nursed both ways. This is particularly important when the baby will receive the bottle from

---

* Cf. Chap. V, Section 6 in The Depths of the Soul.

someone other than his mother and, consequently, might experience a sense of pain at being deprived of the tenderness to which he was accustomed.

It is also very important to examine the nutritive qualities of the milk in the baby bottle: it must be perfectly adapted to the baby's needs. More or less serious traumatic experiences can result from improper or insufficient nutrition at this state. The nipple on his baby bottle represents the first real contact with the outside world (his mother's breast still seems a part of himself to the very young baby), and if this first contact is too painful or unpleasant, the outside world might remain indelibly stamped on his unconscious as a hostile reality. This, in turn, can develop into a narcissistic retreat into self, or even schizoid behavior, throughout the rest of his adult life.

Breaking off too abruptly is always a traumatic experience, it would seem, even more so when the child is still very young and still almost exclusively centered on his relationship with his mother. To his unconscious mind, this looks like a refusal of love, a withholding of the very part of his mother which occupies the whole center of attention in his infant universe. The lack of joy and dynamic approach to living and the feeling of insecurity which so many people suffer are frequently the result of poorly managed weaning. We might well wonder if perhaps the custom that is so prevalent among primitive peoples, and even in some of our own good country people today, of nursing the baby until the age of two or three or even older, does not somehow respond to the deep urgings of some primal instinct within the mother. When the child is nursed over this long period, other foods are generally added to his diet, in addition to his mother's milk, and the transition to other food is generally effected without the least disturbance.

Now, obviously, we do not recommend this practice to every mother. For the majority of them, such a plan would be physsically impossible, to say nothing of the almost equally serious traumatic effects which, in our day and age, could easily result from such a practice. By excessively prolonging this most intimate relationship between baby and mother, the child is over-exposed to the danger of acute fixation on his mother, and consequently will find it much more difficult to adapt to the outside world. The only element to be retained as essential from the practices discussed above is to make the period of weaning as gentle a transition as possible. The more difficult this changing to a new method of nutrition appears to be for the baby, the more lavish his mother must be with her love and caresses and all the other signs of her affection and tenderness. The essential thing for the child, the very source of his future sense of security, of his confidence in life, in self, and in other people, is to know that he is loved.

On the other hand, weaning presents a problem not only for the child, but for his mother. All too often it happens that the mother clings to her child as something that belongs to her. She refuses to let him go; she does not let him begin his own independent existence in a normal fashion. It is true that her child has a great need for her love, but the parents must love the child for his own sake, not their own.

## II. *Cain Complex*

The birth of a young brother or sister can be the source either of joy or sadness for the child: either way it is a very important event in his life. It can be a particularly painful experience for the first-born, since it puts an abrupt end to his privileged position as only child and his exclusive claim upon his mother's care and affection and love.

Louis was two when his brother Alan was born. He was enthusiastic, well behaved, ate what was given him, and seemed not at all disturbed. At first, he welcomed the news that he was going to have a little brother, hoping that the brother would be fun to play with. But little by little, Louis' behavior began to change completely. He started wetting his bed again and became unpredictable and fussy about his food. No longer gay and talkative, he became quiet and moody, completely losing his ability to chatter away about the trifles of his daily existence. His parents discovered that he would secretly try to pinch and bite his little brother, whereas in public he maintained an air of studied and scornful indifference towards him. The punishments he got for this only made the situation worse.

On the advice of a child psychologist, Louis' mother put an end to the punishments. One morning, upon discovering that he had wet his bed again, instead of scolding him, she took him in her lap and hugged him. Then she asked him why he had wet the bed again. "Louis just as little baby as Alan," was his sobbing reply.

The problem here, of course was a very elementary psychological fact. After the lavish affection and attentions he enjoyed as an only child, Louis felt that he was being neglected after the birth of his little brother. The new baby was of delicate health and required much care and attention, and his mother logically enough spent much less time on the "big" brother who was strong and healthy.

With the instinctive logic of small children, Louis could only conclude that he was loved less than before, simply because he was no longer a baby. Since nothing can entirely compensate for a mother's love in the child's young experience, this little child could be expected to see only the disadvantages of growing up and then he went back to the behavior that was expected of him when he was a very young baby.

Louis' sense of frustration upon the birth of his brother was, however, rather mild and benign in form. Many children of his age, or just a little older, have actually been known to try to strangle or suffocate their baby brother or sister, to break or empty his bottle and deprive him of the food he needs, to blame him for little things that they have deliberately done themselves. This type of behavior is called the Cain complex.

Most of the time, regressions to infant behavior, such as the case just described, are not a serious problem at all. The normal child will soon enough rediscover his spontaneous joy in growing up and of his own accord he will grow out of these leftovers from his babyhood. Only through the intervention of other factors, external or internal, will the child tend to have a real fixation on infantile behavior and reaction, and thereby experience inhibitions in the whole of his emotional development. Most adults who behave and react like children have been poorly weaned, that is, poorly loved.

It is obvious that the mother, and generally only the mother, is in a position to keep her child free from any possible fixation on either a weaning complex or what we have called the Cain complex. In this she will need much delicacy and probably some little guidance, since her mother instinct is not enough to see her through so complex and delicate a problem. The essential element is always not so much to make the child know and understand, but rather to make him feel that he is always loved as he was before, notwithstanding the arrival of his little brother or sister. No matter how psychically and physically absorbing her new obligations might prove to be, the mother must do nothing to frustrate her older child in his need to be loved and fondled. In young children, this need is just as fundamental and essential as the need for food and air in any living creature. Thus, she must never push him aside abruptly in order to care for the new baby. If the older child is already three or four years old, and if he is capable of understanding what his mother explains to him, it is an excellent idea to get him actively interested in taking care of the new baby, to associate him as far as possible in the intimacy which necessarily exists between the new baby and the mother. The "big" brother or sister must also feel some of the responsibility for the new baby, so that instead of jealousy, he will experience the legitimate pride of the strong person who is protecting the weak. Let us, however, insist once again on the fact that the mother's action and behavior are infinitely more important than any words of explanation. The first stirrings of emotional life in the young child come to life far in advance of his use of reason and intelligence.

The mother's behavior, no matter how good a teacher she is, will not possibly be exactly the same towards the older child as it is towards the newborn baby. To keep this inevitable difference from looking like a terrible injustice at first, it is necessary for the father to take a more and more important role in the child's life. In order to promote the psychic equilibrium of the child, it is not a healthy attitude to consider his education as the exclusive province of the mother; the father must be involved in this process from the very beginning, as much as possible. If he refuses this role, on the fallacious pretext that this is not a man's work, but a woman's, the mother will almost always be unable to manage the child's education by herself. The child who experiences only his mother's affection and care — whether she be unmarried, widow, divorcee, or simply because the father refuses to share in the task of bringing up his children—will rarely enjoy good psychic health.

However, we must not confuse the sense of frustration a child might experience at the birth of a little brother or sister with the normal rivalry that exists between brothers and sisters in the average family. Such a rivalry not only presents no danger to emotional maturity, and thus has no objectively evil consequences to fear, but is generally a very healthy sign of normalcy. It can serve as a stimulus to growing up, if the parents know how to inculcate this ambition in their children.

As a general rule, it is not a mistake for the first two children to be more or less close in age. As for the children who follow, a longer period of spacing is generally desirable. Children who have bigger brothers and sisters are much more easily stimulated to activity. On the other hand, family rivalries are much less likely to take on dangerous proportions between brothers and sisters who are separated by a few years in age.

### III. *Oedipus Complex*

The presence of his father in his own and his mother's life quite soon presents a difficult emotional problem for the child. Freudian psychology sees this situation as the real pivotal point around which revolves the whole psychological development of the child, either advanced or promoted or seriously impaired by this conflict. According to this theory, the child is in love, sexually in love, with his mother. The father soon takes on the character of a dangerous rival, for the child is quick to notice the intimacy which exists between his parents. Despite the admiration which the child still experiences towards his father, he cannot help hating him as a rival to his mother's love. In most cases, only the love and admiration are conscious, the hate being repressed in the depths of the unconscious. There it gives rise to all sorts of disturbances in the emotional life of the child, more or less seriously vitiating the normal relationship between child and parents.

Initially, the Oedipus complex takes on almost the same form in girls as in boys, according to Freudian theory. But little by little the girl falls in love with her father and thus sees her mother as a rival. This is called the *Electra complex,* and it works in precisely the same manner as the Oedipus complex.

In accord with the almost unanimous opinion of other non-Freudian depth psychologists, we hesitate to adopt this rather mystical and not quite scientific view of things as presented by the Oedipus and Electra complex. This is not to say that this complex does not exist as such in a certain number of neurotic patients. But, up to the present time, no scientifically sound argument has been advanced to demonstrate its universal applicability, neither in the case of established neurotics, nor, all the more, in the greater majority of people who are not psychically unsound. Thus, in accordance with the principles of proper scientific procedure, the Oedipus and Electra complex, like any other scientific hypothesis, must not be presumed as a postulate of psychological experience; it still needs to be individually proved in each particular case.

But what does seem beyond question is the fact that in most families the children will experience a much more pronounced attachment for the parent of the opposite sex. This attachment is, in some cases, more or less exclusive. Sometimes it implies, equivalently, a feeling of jealousy, even open hostility, towards the other parent. Still there is no proof for the specifically sexual nature of this attachment, even in the rather broad sense in which Freudian psychology understands the term. In a good many cases which I have been in a position to observe personally, this sort of preference is only a response to the predilection which the parents themselves, more or less consciously, develop in their children. The father will see in his daughter — and especially in an only daughter among many sons — the fresh new image of the woman he loves. And the mother, in a similar way, is proud of her son.

Such a preference for one particular child among parents in normal and harmonious families is not blameworthy in the least, nor does it present any threat to the psychological maturity of the children. Quite the contrary, it can even make an active contribution towards promoting the emotional development of the children, while at the same time it affords the parents a most intense joy, in recompense for the many sacrifices and cares that are always involved in bringing up a family. It is not uncommon for the husband, through his love for his daughter, to rediscover, a fresh flame of love for his wife that the years of living together somehow managed to obscure in his awareness.

In poorly unified families, things are different. There it is possible for two hostile camps to rise, father and mother both using the special affection from one of their children as a weapon to injure each other. Neither does it do any good to point out the extremely injurious effects of such a family situation for the children.

Anne was a most unfortunate housewife. Her husband disappointed her with his lack of love and she suspected him of infidelity; she felt neglected and unloved. She transferred all her hunger for affection onto her only son. She fondled and embraced him constantly and kept him close to her as much as she possibly could. The boy was ten years old and he still fell asleep every night in his mother's arms. When his father was away, he stayed there all night; other nights he was carried to his own bed when his father retired. Anne always scolded her son for his hostile and jealous attitude towards his father, but it was too obvious, even for the boy, from the very tone of her scolding that deep down inside, she was delighted at his attitude. Without really being conscious of the fact, by her own attitudes and uncontrolled feelings, she was actually nursing this hostility along, especially whenever she happened to notice some sign of admiration for his father in her son. Here, the boy's hatred for his father was largely a mere sharing in his mother's own feeling and attitudes. Such imitative behavior on the part of most children is a very common phenomenon, and it is surprising to note how rapidly they assimilate the emotional reactions and prejudices of their favorite parent.

Anne obviously had a deep-seated fear that her son would one day take after his father, leaving her for some other woman. Consequently, she dressed him like a girl, kept his hair long and curly, and suggested all sorts of sissy games to him. Apart from the possibility of a surprise reaction againt these influences, when the boy has reached adolescence, it is greatly to be feared that he will never be a real man. His strong fixation on his mother will keep him from turning into an adult, and sexually he runs great risk of inversion.

Alexander "had" to get married — his girl-friend was pregnant. She did not belong to his social circle at all, she was completely different from the "girl like mother" that he had dreamed of marrying all during his adolescence. As a result, he did not really love her at all; he devoted all his affection to their oldest daughter, who was a faithful portrait of his own mother. He would not allow his wife to punish or scold the child; whenever she did, he would take the girl on his lap and soothe her and never fail to scold his wife for her behavior. It is not at all surprising that the little daughter will be passionately attached to her father and show a certain hostility towards her mother. She keeps saying that she wants to marry her daddy when she grows up: meantime, she admires and imitates him in every possible way. She will have nothing to do with dolls and the usual girls' games; she wants to play soldiers, she loves automobiles, she likes to go around dressed like a boy — all to the obvious delight of her father. Everything feminine is repugnant to this little girl, because it reminds her of her mother.

Unless this dangerous inclination towards being a boy is neutralized in time (by puberty at very latest), the little girl is in serious danger of repudiating her woman's vocation in life, becoming a "virago" and perhaps even a Lesbian.

These two examples, chosen from thousands of cases, ought to be enough to convince the reader of the immense importance of married harmony in the psychological development of the children.


## IV. Parental Cooperation

For any real success in bringing up the children, the active cooperation of both parents is absolutely necessary. When the father — as is, unfortunately, so frequently the case — refuses to have any part in it, there are always some more or less serious traumatic scars in the child's psyche.

Too much occupied or preoccupied by their professional problems, by their political and social commitments, coming home late every night when the children are already in bed, most men more or less explicitly feel that the raising of the children is the woman's task alone. This opinion might be all right as far as the necessary care for the physical development of the children is concerned. But for their emotional development, all the good-will and all the natural intuition and effort of the mother are not enough to make up for the indispensable element of the father's influence, for girls as well as for boys. The mother belongs too intimately to the narcissistic world of the child. It is only through the intermediary of his father's influence that the child ought to (and normally does) branch out into the outside world: and this is an absolutely necessary condition for growing up. Whenever the father, for any reason whatsoever, is remiss in this duty, the child's contact with the outside world, with everything we generally refer to as reality, is always retarded, and sometimes irrevocably compromised.

Mothers must struggle against the temptation of making their husband assume the role of family policeman, called in only to bolster up their own authority when it is questioned by the child. All too often we see mothers who do not know what to do with their children, or who are afraid, more or less consciously, that they might be losing their children's love, threatening to "tell daddy when he comes home." They want their husband to be severe, to be docile in executing the verdict they themselves have pronounced over the child's misbehavior. Such an attitude in a mother is extremely prejudicial to establishing a true intimacy between the children and their father — an intimacy which is already complicated by enough obstacles and difficulties of its own.

For the children's own best good, both tenderness and

punishment when necessary, ought to be the work of both parents, even when it is actually only the father or mother alone who is active in a particular case. The child needs to know that he is equally loved by both parents, and this can never be the case if it is always the one who hugs and kisses him and the other who spanks him and scolds him. There is much common sense in the old pedagogical principle, still in vogue in many middle-class families, that children ought never to be aware of any discord between their parents.

## V. Rewards and Punishments

The experienced psychologist is hardly in a position to share Rousseau's optimistic view regarding the radical goodness of human nature. Such a position would condemn, *a priori*, the very principle of rewards and punishment in bringing up children.

A good many educators have shown a tendency to condemn corporal punishment without appeal, regarding it as the primary cause of a number of psychic traumas. Nothing in my experience as a practicing psychologist can authorize such an out-of-hand condemnation, as far as mental hygiene is concerned. Punishment, corporal or moral, could present only one real psychological danger to the child, namely that of making him feel that he is not loved. But this can happen only through the fault of the parents, especially when they punish him in anger, or when the child has fully understood the justice of the punishment. In this respect, a harsh word or the simple denial of some dessert after dinner can be just as harmful as a slap or a spanking. But when the parents have managed to make their child understand that the punishment he is receiving is in proportion to his misbehavior, then corporal punishment is often much more effective than, for example, being deprived of a dessert or a Sunday afternoon at the movies, punishments which run the risk of doing much more damage to his equilibrium and health.


## VI. Over-affectionate Mothers

Whatever the role that the father plays in the psychological development of his children, beginning even with the child's pre-existence in the womb, it is always the mother who, in a quite different way, makes the principal contribution to this development. Mental hygiene is always, in some degree, an integrating part of her married and social responsibility, at least as important as hygiene of the body. Unfortunately though, whereas the principles and techniques of bodily hygiene are familiar to practically every mother in our day and age, the principles and techniques of psychological hygiene are unknown to the majority of parents.

We make no mention here of those misguided mothers who systematically mistreat or refuse to love their children, or some particular one of their children. Notwithstanding the publicity such mothers receive in the press which caters to the sensational, their number is, happily, very small. And even that number is made up, generally, of "unfortunates," victims of drink or dope or other vices.

The vast majority of women unquestionably love their children and their devotion to their children very frequently rises to the level of the sublime. Still it all too frequently happens that these same mothers do very great harm to their children and are a more or less serious factor in inhibiting their emotional maturity, thus shackling them with a severe handicap for their later life. If it is true that love is a natural outburst of the human heart, and especially of a mother's heart, it is more difficult than we might imagine to love properly. It even seems probable that those mothers who are tender and affectionate towards their children do them greater harm than those who love them less tenderly. The greater number of neurotics who visit their psychologist or psychiatrist have had a mother who was too loving. As a general rule, such mothers are quite taken up with their own neurotic problems and, because of their own problems, they love their children, not for their children's sake, but for their own.

Marie-Therese was 25 years old when she went to see the psychologist. She wanted to marry, because she could see no meaning in her life outside marriage. But the least contact with a man always threw her into a veritable panic. If even a friend of the family or a passer-by spoke a few words to her or even looked directly at her, her heart would start beating violently, she would blush profusely, and begin to stutter when she spoke. How could she possibly get married?

The psychologist was not long in observing that Marie-Therese had a mother who loved her passionately. Her mother did everything possible to spare her every painful shock, to protect her against every danger. Even now her mother did not like her to take the train alone, or the neighborhood bus. Disillusioned in her marriage, she had involuntarily inspired her daughter with a real fear of men — she spoke of men as if they were the worst evil that her daughter could encounter in all her life. Still this did not keep her mother from being concerned about her daughter's failure to marry. It is only that the mother wanted to make her own choice of a future son-in-law. Whenever she spoke about her future son-in-law, it was easy to see that she wanted someone as different as possible from her own husband, Marie-Therese's father. If the psychologist had had an opportunity to treat the mother, he would doubtless have discovered that, actually, she had no desire at all for her daughter to marry, but wanted to keep her home for good. Since her husband had refused his love, probably because she was too insistent upon being loved, the only reason for living now was to watch over her daughter as if she had never stopped being a baby. In order to hold on to this justification of her existence, she had easily enough managed to maneuver her daughter into a position in which she was psychologically incapable of any intimacy with a man. Convinced that her daughter, just like her mother, was a "pearl of great price," she no doubt experienced a measure of satisfaction in refusing her daughter to all men, and thus taking vengeance on her own husband.

If so many children experience such great difficulty in growing into adults, it is almost always due to the fact that their mother — without being aware of it, most of the time — did everything she could to keep them babies, that is, in a state of absolute dependence on their mother. Psychologically, the mother will not admit that the umbilical cord has been severed. The least desire for independence on the child's part is considered as an unbearable act of disobedience, and reprimanded as an evidence of bad will. Frequently, mothers like this will continue to dress their children like babies, up to an age where, normally, the child would want to be more like a grown-up. They fear for their child constantly; every possible mistake, every possible slip, every time he has a little sore, and quickly turn their child into a real "scaredy-cat."

On the other hand, some mothers lavish such affection on their children because they themselves feel that they are to blame for the situation in the family. This is particularly the case with divorced or remarried women. Their unconscious sense of guilt leads them into serious mistakes in an attempt to make good the harm that has been done in depriving their children of their father.

As far as mental hygiene is concerned it is a thousand times better for the child to be too bold rather than too timid. On both the physical and the moral plane, mistakes and sins are infinitely less serious in their consequences than the absence of all initiative in the child. For fear that the baby will fall and injure his head on the floor, when he tries to walk should the mother keep her baby from taking his first step? Mothers who insist on walking their 7 or 8 year old to school every morning subject him to a painful humiliation in front of his classmates and companions. The psychic dangers which result from such humiliation are certainly much more serious than the supposed physical dangers that the mother wants to keep him from by walking him to school. To be sure, it is always possible that the child will lose his way: but this happens only rarely and most of the time, after moments of wandering about, he will rediscover the right way by himself. But by keeping too close a guard over her son, the mother can easily give him a serious inferiority complex which will be a grave problem during his whole adult life.

I know some intelligent parents who let their children ride the neighborhood bus alone at the age of 8, to visit friends who live in another part of town. This obviously involves some element of risk, even though the child feels very proud of the trust his parents show for him, even though he is happy to be treated "like a grown-up," and obviously does his best to deserve their confidence and trust. There need be no fear that such a child will refuse to grow up, that he will be tempted to suffer any fixation on the infantile stage.

It goes without saying that children must not be allowed these little responsibilities all of a sudden, overnight. If a child who had always been treated like a baby were suddenly allowed to ride the bus all alone, he would probably experience a sense of anxiety which would do him great harm and he would be in some danger of making a blunder that might seriously influence his emotional development. Even just crossing the street might prove to be dangerous in this respect for children who have been too sheltered. The child's progressive initiation to the proper use of freedom and responsibility must begin very early in his formation.

## VII. The Immature Mother

A neurotic mother, that is, a mother who is emotionally immature, is always very poor at bringing up her children. As a rule, she only helps to make her children neurotics like herself. This is because she is incapable of acting like an adult towards them and, as a result, lets herself be drawn into their own childish conflicts.

Mrs. N. had two children, aged 11 and 7. She complained bitterly over their lack of obedience, their poor table manners, and it hurt her to realize that she had neither authority nor prestige in their eyes. The psychologist quickly discovered that the cause of this unfortunate state of affairs was Mrs. N's own emotional immaturity. She could not keep from joining in their games and thus was constantly involved in the conflicts which are so characteristic of children's games. Whenever one of her daughters acted counter to what her mother, then and there, considered right and proper, she saw it as a personal offense and lost all her good spirits. The punishments she inflicted were not at all in proportion with the objective gravity of the wrong they had done; they were measured by the intensity of the offense she felt herself. Thus it would happen, that, according to her mood, the same behavior on the part of her children would one day be received not only with indulgence but even with a sort of juvenile complicity, whereas the next day it would likely be punished with excessive severity: verbal and physical punishment would rain down on the "guilty parties." As a result, her little girls considered their mother as a "scatterbrain" and paid no attention to her opinions and decisions.

This is not to say that Mrs. N's children did not love their emotionally immature mother. Quite the contrary, on certain days they showed her many signs of love and affection. But this affection always took on a protective or condescending tone. They loved her like a little sister, like someone weak who did not know what she was doing. And at the same time they were unconsciously exposed to the contagion of their mother's emotional immaturity. It was hard for them to walk along the path to maturity with any real confidence; they were deprived of that indispensable guidance which only a mother can fully supply. For them, their mother was not the incarnation of an ideal self who could lead them on towards the discovery of the adult world. Rather, she could easily give them such a distorted picture of this world that growing up held no attraction for the children.

This example is obviously a rather extreme case. But there are still a good many mothers, less neurotic along these lines than Mrs. N., who have no idea how to behave like adults towards their children. Thus they are a traumatic influence on the very ones they want to protect and help.

Mrs. D., the young mother of a Protestant and intellectual family, was diametrically opposed to Mrs. N. in her conduct towards the children. She spoke to them as if they were adults; she expounded on her philosophical and religious theories. This, too, was not without its dangers. Mrs. D's children experienced a very precocious maturity of mind which kept them from having their full share in the simpler games and joys of childhood. A degree of psychic imbalance could easily result. It is dangerous to inhibit the child's desire to be an adult; it is not a good idea either to let this desire become so ardent that the child skips some of the normal stages of development.

Unconsciously, the child expects to see his parents show him an example of the values and ideals that they are trying to inculcate in him. He finds it discouraging to admit that his parents demand a sort of perfection from him that they do not practice themselves. In paraphrase of Beaumarchais, Doctor André Berge writes: "In view of the virtues we demand of our children, do you know very many parents who deserve to be children?"*

## VIII. The Child Understands Almost Everything ...

Far too frequently, parents will discuss their own conflicts, problems and difficulties in front of their children. On the pretext that the children are "too small to understand," they hold nothing back in their quarreling and arguments. Such conduct can lead to serious danger for the psychic equilibrium of the children.

Because the child is too young to understand certain things in an intellectual way, many parents conclude, and quite wrongly, that such things have no influence on the child at all. But the child's unconscious keeps a record of a vast number of facts and impressions which completely escape his conscious perception; this data is no less harmful, in his unconscious, merely because he is not consciously aware of its presence.

Mathilda, a nervous and frequently very sad child, eleven years old, told the Sister at school: "If I am almost always sad, that is because I don't have a mommy. I have a hollow place here in my heart that comes from never being loved."

The Sister did not understand how such a young girl can think such a thing, especially since she knew Mathilda's mother was still living. And when Mathilda's mother learned of what her daughter had told the good Sister, she was very proud to have "such an intelligent child."

Actually there is absolutely nothing in Mathilda's reactions that offers any evidence of her intelligence. Her mother was quite neurotic and for several years she had been undergoing psychological treatment. When Mathilda was only seven or

---

*Le Métier de Parent, p. 77 (Editions Montaigne)

eight years old, her mother used to discuss her own neurotic problems, in her presence, with her husband. She always dwelt particularly on what, thanks to the psychoanalysis, she was discovering about her fundamental problem, which was her relationship with her father as a young girl. Her father had been very hard to get along with and had never shown the least sign of affection for her: she always spoke of "never having had a real father." Mathilda's unconscious, to which no one paid the least attention, had kept a record of all these conversations which her conscious mind could not recall in any way. With a child's penchant for imitating, she was naturally enough expressing herself in exactly the same way that her mother did.

The serious danger here is the fact that such "convictions" in the child easily turn into neurosis. Convinced that her mother does not love her, which is equivalent to saying that she does not have any mother, the child begins to behave as if, actually, she did not have a mother.

We can never be sufficiently on guard against the *neurogenic* powers of auto-suggestion and mimetism in the child. That is why it is so important for parents to be very careful in everything they say in front of their children, even when the children are still very young.

## IX. *Overcompensation on the Parent's Part*

More or less consciously, some parents (nor can it be said, in their defense, that they are particularly neurotic themselves), tend to compensate, in their children, for what they feel was most sadly wanting in their own childhood.

Charles had to suffer a good deal, during his childhood, from his father's over-severity. Divorced and remarried, the father used to strike him regularly and subject him to an almost military regime of discipline. As for his step-mother, she never showed any sign of love or affection for the sensitive boy, obviously preferring her own children in every way. If this lack of love throughout his childhood did not make Charles a neurotic, he owes his good fortune to his healthy stock and to the sublimation he discovered, very early in childhood, in an intense spiritual life.

When he married in his turn, and became the father of a family, Charles was afraid to impose any restrictions on his children, and he never punished them. Still, he was concerned about their naughty behavior; they were noisy and hard to amuse; they would break or soil everything that fell into their hands. On the conscious plane, Charles justified his attitude by a process of rationalization, in terms of some very questionable theories of child psychology which prescribe a maximum of freedom for the child, without any restraints on his behavior. Actually, it was his unconscious that was driving him to overcompensate, in his own children, for what he missed most of all when he was a child.

The most regrettable element of all such unconscious overcompensation is the fact that it leads to the opposite excess. The almost anarchical freedom that Charles' children enjoyed threatens to involve them in consequences that will be at least as serious as the excessive constraint which marred his own childhood. There is, in fact, great fear that his children will find it most difficult to adapt to the discipline and inhibitions which they will inevitably encounter at school and later on in their jobs and social relations.

When Marcella was still a little girl, her mother, a society woman, left her almost completely to herself. The child was generally poorly dressed and dirty and the children she played with used to pick on her for this reason. When she was barely ten, she was violated by two boys who were some years older. She felt that it was a sort of miracle that she did not turn into a real street-walker or at least a problem teen-ager. She did very well in her studies and married "well," and was now the mother of a charming daughter, Chantal, eight years old. She kept Chantal with her all the time and scrubbed and dressed her like a deluxe doll. She hardly ever allowed her to play with the other children, for fear that she would have to face the same humiliations and dangers that her mother knew as a young child. In a word, Marcella was doing everything she could to to make her daughter's world as radically different as possible from the world she had known herself.

It is not difficult to predict that, in this process of over-compensation, Marcella, is going to end up doing just as much to her daughter as she had suffered at the hands of her own mother. I would not go so far as to say, with some psycho-analysts, that Marcella and Charles are unconsciously taking vengeance on their children for their own sufferings in childhood. But it is equally obvious that, objectively, the result of this conduct will be a sort of vengeance. It is good to compensate, but very dangerous to overcompensate.

## X. The Child at School

One of the most important events in the life of the child occurs when he leaves for school. Most children will suffer at being separated from their mother and home all day long. The child almost always starts out by experiencing a certain difficulty in adapting to this new milieu. There are a host of new people there who greet him with indifference if not with open hostility. He is no longer the "dear little darling;" he no longer hears the terms of endearment or nicknames that he hears at home; he goes by his first name or his family name. Among his schoolmates there are some who are not well brought up and, as if by fate it is they who lead the others. "Bright" children, only sons or only daughters, are quite upset by the atmosphere of the school.

As a general rule, however, the innate instinct of sociability will compensate the child for these inconvenient and uncomfortable elements in his new experience. Normally, the school, despite the discipline that flourishes there, manages to satisfy the child's normal need to escape from the circle of family relationships which has now grown too narrow. Thus it looks as if he is being set free and at the same time prompted.

Children who have begun going to school rather early frequently experience less difficulty in adapting to adulthood and the demands of social living than those who have been taught at home, either by a governess or a sort of home-study course. Parents who prefer this last method of instruction instead of sending their children to school, are making a big mistake. Contrary to what they think, formal instruction is not the only, nor even the most important, task of the school: the school has to help the child through the very important time of transition from family life to social life.

It is still true that, unless certain elementary precautions are taken, the child's departure for school can be a traumatic experience and contribute to the formation or aggravation of the common "weaning complex" which we have described above. This is a particularly real danger in the case of those children who are very attached to their parents and particularly to their mother. Brutally snatched away from this intimacy, the child will experience a strong anxiety of insecurity, which threatens to be a serious shock to his psychic equilibrium. An only child will find himself exposed to this danger more than others, as will a child who is too strictly forbidden to play with children outside his own narrow social circle, under pretext of keeping him from evil influences. Such children frequently experience much more pain in adapting to the give and take of school life; they are more likely to be picked on by their schoolmates and this in turn can easily result in an inferiority complex.

In order to keep school from being a traumatic experience for the child, the mother should very early begin to promote the child's natural desires for independence and sociability. It should never be necessary for her to ask how she is to "untie her child from her apron strings." The child has an innate instinct to be free of his mother. If he is slow in doing so, it is always his mother's fault; more or less consciously she has prevented him from learning how to fly on his own.

Obviously, it is much easier to prevent these unhappy consequences of improper upbringing by proper training than it is to correct them later. But such mistakes are not at all infrequent, and we must find some way to emancipate the child whose mother has kept him in a state of dependence that is really proper only for babies who are still being nursed.

The parting from the mother must never be the occasion of any brutality. This could give the child the impression that he was being sent off to school simply because he was no longer wanted at home — and the language of emotion would translate this feeling into words we have seen before: "Mommy doesn't love me any more." When the child's fixation on his mother is abnormally strong, a child psychologist is the only answer. In less serious cases, the mother is perfectly capable of seeing this second "weaning process" through to a happy conclusion without too much effort. It would be well for her to do something about the problem as soon as she is aware of it. She should teach the child to be away from her gradually, progressively to play with other children in the neighborhood.

In this work, the father can play a very helpful role. By paying a little more attention to his child, he will be a great aid in breaking down this unfortunate fixation on the mother, or at very least he will no longer be so readily disregarded by the child.

In order to make it easier for the child to adapt to school life, the parents must not consider their children as property belonging to themselves, but rather as autonomous persons. In theory, this ought to go without saying, but every psychologist realizes how hard it is to put all this advice into practice.

Other important psychological problems threaten the child

at the beginning of his school life. It is true that his individual personality must be respected from the most tender age, and that care must always be taken not to load him down with ready-made ideas and norms for conduct. It is particularly indispensable now, at this crisis of his youthful experience, to take into account all the tastes and capacities that make up the personal rhythm of his work and living. Some children have slow minds. They can easily be made to feel inferior if too much work is expected of them, too rapidly. How many children who have been called "lazy" have actually lost their taste for work simply because their instructors did not care (or know) how to evaluate the particular and individual temper of their intelligence, from the very first days of their formal education. The young scholar who constantly misbehaves will more generally need a visit to a competent psychologist than punishment by his parents or his teachers who do not understand the reasons for his behavior. Frequently, an examination will reveal the presence of some unconscious blocks that inhibit his natural curiosity and make study distasteful for him.

I knew John when he was six. He was enrolled in one of those private schools in which the child is asked to repeat only when the parents demand it (and this happens rarely, since most parents are quite willing to believe in their children's natural genius). He had barely managed to make second grade, but he understood hardly anything that he had been taught for that year. However, John was a very intelligent lad: this could be easily discovered by asking him about something in which he was interested. Still, because of his rather slow mind, little inclined towards abstract thinking, he let himself be convinced, at the age of ten, because of the awkward way in which his parents were handling the situation, that he was an imbecile, and that he never would amount to anything in his studies. Thus since he considered school work as a waste of time, he made no effort and managed to learn hardly anything. The insidious element in this case was the fact that his parents went blandly about almost bragging that they could see nothing but failure in store for their son, when it was they, themselves, who were largely to blame for his condition: they were the ones who discouraged their son.

Experience proves that with good will and the proper approach it is possible to make each and every child take an interest in his school work, unless he is an absolute idiot. And the very first condition for success in his studies is interest in what he is being taught. In an effort to stimulate such an interest, there is no point in preaching a sermon to the child. The more his parents insist, the more the child will give in to his spontaneous tendency to believe that it is his parents he is working for at school. He will, of course, be willing to work very hard if the desire to please his parents is dominant in him, but, on the other hand, when his unconscious mind harbors some trace of hostility towards them (and this is frequently the case), he will do poor work, in order to get even with them or make them upset.

Since perseverance in school work is not a frequent virtue among children, parents will obviously have to watch what their children are studying, and see to it that their homework is not neglected. But here too, the parents must use extreme discretion in the exercise of their duty: otherwise they might kill the natural initiative in their child. As for his teachers, it is contrary to every sound psychological and educational principle to assign school work or memorization as a punishment.

In the first place, this only confirms the child in his conviction that he is working for adults. And besides, as experience has shown, the child's unconscious frequently has some secret reason of his own for wanting to be punished: this will be an added motive for poor work at school.

## XI. " Too Grown-up"

There are some parents who have almost an obsession for making their children "grown-up."

For this reason they train their children to behave like dogs on show. They expect their children to be always impeccably proper, never noisy, to speak when they are spoken to, etc. Such discipline generally ends up choking out any natural spontaneity and, finally, in stifling the child's personality. The temperament and natural dynamism of some children lends itself very poorly to such "grown-up" conduct. To avoid punishment or win a word of praise from their parents, they turn into hypocrites and liars.

Most of the time the child will turn to lying as the only possible way to defend his own personality. In this respect, it is very important not to confuse the imaginative tales and story-telling of which some children are so fond, with real objective lying: the principal distinguishing characteristic being that the lie always offers some advantage to the child.

Parents must understand that the urge to follow his own initiative is almost as essential to the normal maturity of their child as his need for security and love. A mother or father does not have to be a psychologist or professional educator to realize that children who are forced to be too "grown-up" will usually turn into smart alecks, show-offs, and loud-mouths. In later life, many more of them will end up in need of psychotherapy than those who were real "devils" when they were children.

Obviously, any system of education that deserves the name will have great respect for social norms and good manners and proper etiquette. What we are protesting against here, in the name of mental hygiene, is the error of overdeveloping this area and making it central in the formation of the child.

Diametrically opposed to the too grown-up child is the "difficult" child. As a youngster, he resists every attempt at inculcating habits of personal cleanliness. Wetting, and even soiling, his pants continues much longer than normal in his case. He makes a lot of noise and tries to break anything he can get his hands on. When he has nothing else to tear up, he will scratch himself with his fingernails — a sort of self-destruction. When he gets bigger, he shows traits of disobedience and stubbornness, constant bickering with his brothers and sisters and classmates at school.

His parents should not be too alarmed at this. They make an even bigger mistake if they think that the best way to treat difficult children is to trick them or reason with them. In their desire to correct the situation, they must always remember that difficult children are almost always children *in difficulty*. The only way to really help them is to solve their difficulty.

The baby's refusal to learn proper toilet training from his mother or nurse almost always has some emotional reason behind it. Rightly or wrongly, the child feels neglected, and he soils himself so that his parents will have to pay some attention to him. He can never be helped out of this feeling by being humiliated or shamed. Quite the contrary; he will notice that those around him pay a good deal of attention to his misbehavior and this will only make him deeper rooted in his habits. He would rather be a naughty child and draw attention than a good child and go unnoticed. Only a very gentle and understanding attitude on the part of the mother can succeed in making the child prefer obedience to attention. "The difficult child," as Dr. André Berge judiciously remarks, "is a child whose will, consciously or otherwise, is in conflict with the will of those around him." This is a conflict that needs to be resolved.

The situation is not essentially different in the case of older children, particularly when they reach school age. None of their faults or failings will yield to punishment or humiliation. The only way to cure the unruly or untidy or dishonest school-age child is to win his confidence. He must be given responsibilities: maintaining order in the class or looking out for the weak and smaller children. He must be made to feel enthusiasm for some hero or model he can imitate. Nor must his parents ever forget that most of the people who have accomplished something really worth while with their lives were difficult children when they were young. They had a chance to overcome their difficulties without being turned into "smart alecks".

## XII. Need for Love and Respect

The child is never simply passive. It is not enough for him to be the object of tenderness and love. Nor, for that matter, is it absolutely necessary for his parents to lavish kisses and embraces upon their child in order to give him a feeling of security. In some cases, excess in this area can give rise to an infantile fixation which will impede the child's necessary emancipation as he matures. In his book, *Inhibition, Symptoms, Anxieties,* Freud makes the very important point that "spoiling the child is a practice which tends to unduly prolong his infancy, an age which is characterized by both motor and psychic undevelopment." I know many families who have never made it a practice to hug their children each morning and night, each time they leave or come back home, and still there is a noticeable atmosphere of affection there: the children know that they are loved and secure.

As a general rule, however, a minimum of external show of affection is still desired to promote the emotional development of the child. When such manifestations are lacking, it is much more difficult to make the child feel the love his parents have for him.

André, a teacher, had a poorly adjusted need to please his students, to please everyone he met. He even humiliated himself and made himself ridiculous in order to achieve this goal. But he usually went about this in such an awkward way that instead of loving him (for that is what he was actually looking for), people ran away from him. He was most unhappy as a result, and ended up by believing in neither love nor friendship. He had dreamed of marrying a tender and loving woman: in fact he had been searching for such a wife all his life long. But the quirks of fortune made him marry a cousin who was alone and without resources after the death of her father for whom she had cared during his old age: he married out of sense of duty, not for love. His wife was plain, mannish, outspoken and dour: he had no feeling of real affection for her at all. Poor André was not ever loved, and he loved only in his dreams.

In the course of the psychotherapy which he underwent after a serious crisis of depression, it turned out that André's parents, though they had been very good people, had never managed to express their affection for him in any outward sign or gesture. As a little boy he had frequently envied the other little boys whose mothers used to hug and embrace them in the public parks. His parents were very reserved and made a cult of duty: they felt it was proof enough of their affection if they were concerned about André's health and sent him off to school at great personal sacrifice to themselves. They would have gladly faced death for their son but it never even entered their mind that what they somewhat disdainfully referred to as "sentimental affection" was just as important for their child as the nourishment his body demanded.

It was this frustration over having experienced no outward expression of love, in his early childhood that made André go out of his way to look for signs of friendship and interest on the part of his parents, and he was acting out of a "sense of duty" when he married. And yet, more than anywhere else, it was in his marriage that he hoped to discover the tenderness and affection that he missed so much.

Emotional development, in the child, requires not only that the child feel loved, but also that he be able to love and respect others. The first object of this love and respect is, of course, his parents.

At the age of four or five, the child, in a confused way, experiences the need of a living model to serve as his ideal. In tending towards identification with his ideal, he gradually comes to form his own personality, in the midst of a riot of manifold impulses from within, and problems and trials from without.

The worst misfortune that can befall a child is to be deceived by someone whom, instinctively, he has taken for the perfect model of his own life's ambitions. The threat of such a disillusion is even more serious when the heroic image that the child builds of his own father or mother is to be found, not in the world of reality, but in story books and the history of the past. Inevitably the child will someday realize that his father bears no real resemblance to Ulysses or St. Francis, that his mother is not really very much like the Blessed Virgin or a movie star.

When this inevitable disillusionment takes place gradually, progressively, and in step with the child's developing sense of reality, although it will always be a painful enough experience for the child, only rarely will it lead to really serious consequences. Infinitely more traumatic is the discovery that even on the plane of reality his parents do not deserve his respect or merit his esteem.

Dorothy, a young married woman, went to see the psychologist because she was frigid and her husband had threatened to leave her. It gradually developed that frigidity, as well as her habitual sadness and almost complete lack of interest and taste for life, both had one very definite common root. When Dorothy was about seven, the door between her bedroom and her parents' room was left open and she was awakened by the racket her father made coming home drunk one night. Her mother, clad only in her nightgown, was trying to calm her husband down, but he threw her down on the bed and, while she sobbed with humiliation, he threw himself on top of her. Dorothy soon forgot this terrible scene, but in her unconscious the concept of sex relations was always associated with thoughts of drunkenness, brutality, and violence. Her disinterest in life, after that night's experience took on the form of a total loss of respect for a father whom she had adored up to that time.

## XIII. Sexual Development in the Child

On the subject of infantile sexuality, Dr. Freud had at least as many correct ideas as false ones. It is absurd and the result of a resolutely anti-scientific dogmatism to confuse sexual pleasure with the pleasure the child experiences in sucking his mother's breast, or in the processes of elimination. Nor is there any grounds for seeing a sexual origin in the complex emotional reactions of the child towards his father and mother.

Still, it is an established fact that infantile sexuality does exist. By ignoring it or handling it in the wrong way the parents can possibly give rise to an irremediable deviation in the emotional life of the man or woman into whom their child will one day grow up.

Normally, in very young children, sexuality exists in a purely virtual state, just like freedom, intelligence, the gift of speech, and all the other characteristics of the human species that come into active use only progressively, and sometimes only at adult age.

Between the ages of three and six most children give evidence of a lively curiosity regarding their own sexual organs and those of others. They become interested in the anatomical differences between boys and girls, in the mystery of birth. Between the ages of six and ten, sexuality, even as the mere preoccupation described above, is latent once again, until it reappears, with renewed vigor, at the age of puberty.

Still it can happen, especially in the case of children who are predisposed to neurosis by a series of factors that are rooted in the make-up of the family, that sexual activity will appear much earlier in forms that are remarkably similar to those of adult sexuality. Some boys experience a true erection of the penis while they are still being nursed. It is not rare, particularly in rural regions where the children are very early introduced to sexual union among animals, for little boys of three to six years to try to insert their penis into the vagina or anus of little girls of the same age: and many of these little girls will allow this without any show of resistance. At about this same age, many other children frequently masturbate and sometimes even experience orgasm.

In all these cases, the proper parental reaction poses an extremely delicate problem. Since, in their own minds, the idea of sex is almost always closely bound up with the idea of guilt, the parents are inclined to exaggerate the moral gravity of this precocious sexual development that they discover in their own children Reprimands and punishment inevitably create a close association between sex and guilt in the child's psyche. Frigidity, importance, perversion, and a more or less serious anxiety, at adult age, can easily result from such an attitude on the part of the parents.

Obviously it is not our intention to recommend that parents approve and encourage such sexual exploration on the part of their children. We only mean to insist on this one lesson from experience, that the only effective way to avoid the dangers that might easily result is not to dramatize the situation. Most of the classic formulas for correcting such activity in children are much more dangerous for the child's psychic equilibrium than the evil they hope to remedy.

At any price, a mother must never threaten her little child that she will "cut it off if he doesn't stop touching himself." The parents obviously do not dream of making the threat good; in their eyes it is only harmless exaggeration intended to make a point. But the child will not understand it in that light: for him it is something deadly serious and the results might well be disastrous for his future development. A great many victims of importance and sex inversion are the result of this famous *castration complex*. This complex, while it certainly does not play so important a role in the child's psychic life as Freudian theory claims, does still present problems too serious for it to be trifled with or ignored. The little sisters of the boy so threatened must also be taken into account. They will actually be inclined to deduce, from hearing such a threat, that they have already undergone this very punishment themselves, and this contributes greatly to a paralyzed feeling of inferiority.

If the parents are not able to dissuade their child from masturbation, then rather than punish him, it would be better simply to close their eyes. Except for pathological cases where a doctor or psychologist has to be consulted, there is every likelihood that around the age of seven the child will stop the habit spontaneously. At that age his primary interests tend to turn towards the outside world and, until the age of puberty, the question of sex will no longer interest him.

One imporatnt factor is this: masturbation is much more frequent among children who do not feel loved. By loving their children properly parents will be able to help them most effectively in this area.

During this same period between the ages of three and six, most children ask some questions about sexual matters, questions which embarrass very many parents who feel incapable of giving an adequate answer.

Obviously it would be absurd to attempt an explanation that the child is not yet capable of following and which, by this very fact, could only have disastrous effects on his sensitivities. Still it is just as important to hold scrupulously fast to the practice of never telling a lie when the child asks, "Where do babies come from? How are they made?" The answers must be true, adapted to their level of understanding, and given without any cause for embarrassment.

Play and games have a major role in the emotional development of the child. Playing with dolls helps little girls to develop their sense of femininity, while playing with tools and playing cowboys helps the boys become aware of their manhood. And, conversely, when little boys play with dolls or when little girls play boys' games, this can be the beginning of serious sexual deviation.

Children, writes Freud, at the approach of the latent period, experience an intellectual regression: they become more awkward and lose their physical grace. Parents must not be alarmed at this: at the age of puberty they will rediscover the gifts and charms they had before the age of reason. Unless, of course, a total ignorance of the rule of mental hygiene has resulted in blocking the development of their emotional impulses.

## XIV. Conclusion

We hope that we have not minimized the dangers which threaten the human personality during the tender years of early childhood. By being well aware of them we shall be better prepared to take them into account. But we must also be on guard against the opposite mistake. Parents and other educators must not let themselves be too taken up with the dangers of neurosis which threaten their children. When educators are not sufficiently endowed with a critical attitude, reading psychological and pedagogical books can have really catastrophic results.

A certain young mother had heard of the evils of repressing her child's initiative, let her little boy do anything he pleased without the least constraint, for fear that she might be repressing his natural instincts and leading him to neurotic complexes.

It is important to understand, as we point out in *The Depths of the Soul*,* that a certain degree of repression of instinctive impulses is absolutely indispensable for the formation of human personality. Too much attention to the prospect of avoiding every possible neurosis frequently leads to the most dangerous results of all.

Parents must try to love their children as well as they possibly can. They must avoid injustice and whim in their own conduct. Above all, they must inspire their children with a real desire to grow up. In order to accomplish this last objective, they must make life appear, not as a path strewn with obstacles but rather as an absorbing adventure.

---

* Especially Chap. X, sec. VI.

# 3 adolescence

## I. The Ungrateful Age

Adolescence stands out as a period of transition from childhood to adult age. It begins with puberty and, in countries that enjoy a temperate climate, it lasts from 12 to 16 in girls and from 13 or 14 to about 18 in boys. By definition the adolescent is a hybrid being: he is no longer a child, but neither is he an adult.

From the physiological point of view, puberty is defined as the capacity to procreate. Its arrival is marked, in girls, by the appearance of their first menstrual periods, and, in boys, by spontaneous or deliberate emission of the semen. This process of ejaculation does not operate with such regularity as menstruation, and consequently the advent of puberty is harder to pinpoint in boys than in girls. But for our purposes in discussing mental health, the exact date of puberty has no particular importance anyhow.

The psychologist realizes that adolescence is a much more complex and complicated reality than mere arrival at the age of puberty. The advent of puberty is, more or less, one single experience, whereas adolescence is really an "age", extending over several years. During this time, profound transformations are taking place within the psyche. Whereas puberty appears as a crisis, adolescence is a long series of crises.

The sexual transformation of the individual is the most obvious mark of puberty. But all throughout the course of adolescence there is a progressive passage from childhood to maturity, a transition which is bound up with significant metamorphoses on the emotional and intellectual plane as well as on the physiological plane. To say that it is sexual maturity that conditions the others is to follow a postulate of psychological insight that experience is unable to establish or confirm.

The adolescent, who, at the outset, is not, psychologically speaking, much different from the child, will not yet enjoy his full intellectual and emotional maturity at the end of his adolescence. It is rather his potential for development that is beginning to stir in the course of these critical years, and it is this potential, and the lines that it begins to follow out in his experience, that will channel his self-realization for the rest of his adult life. If a boy or girl does not experience a capacity or taste for, let us say, mathematics by the age of sixteen or seventeen, it is extremely unlikely that such a capacity will begin to show up later on. On the other hand, it is not infrequent for tastes and talents that appeared very obvious during childhood to disappear completely in the course of adolescence, while new tastes and talents come to light. The same is true in the area of emotional life. It is the child's adolescent years that see the formation of the principal outlines of his behavior towards himself, his parents, and the outside world. These same years decide his orientation towards homo- or hetero-sexuality.

The maturity towards which adolescence ought to lead the individual, throughout the course of its many crises, is fundamentally marked by what can be called *ethical autonomy*. Whereas the child labors under a set of laws and rules which have been imposed by a will other than his own, the adolescent is more in a position to make use of his own judgment and make his own choices in some way. Not that he will necessarily reject the laws and principles which are held up by his family and social surroundings, but he has the conviction, exaggerated at times, that he is acting freely. His judgment becomes more sure; he becomes aware not only of what he does or does not do, of what he wants or does not want, but, equally, and with growing awareness, of the consequences of his acts and desires: he is becoming responsible.

On the emotional plane, adolescence is marked primarily by the development of his capacity for oblative love (outgoing love). It is true, of course, that the child already knows how to love. But his love is almost exclusively in-giving, egocentric, if not even selfish: he demands the care and affection of his mother without ever considering that she might be tired, or have something more urgent to do. The adolescent begins to love others not only for *himself* but also for *themselves*. At least in his imagination, his love will often take on the form of total self-giving to the person he loves.

Psychologists who are more or less orthodox Freudians in their thinking, have a tendency to minimize the role of the psyche. Convinced that the psyche has received its determination exclusively in the emotional experiences of early childhood, they proceed on the principle that nothing really new could possibly be added during adolescence, and that adolescence can do no more than put the finishing touches on the tendencies which already exist. In their eyes, accordingly, mental hygiene has a very restricted field of activity in adolescence.

This position is obviously much exaggerated. It is contradicted by the universal experience of almost all peoples and the practices of almost all religions. Everywhere there is some ceremony to mark the arrival of puberty, the psychological and physiological evidence of the transition from childhood to adolescence, as a major event. This is the time for the child's initiation into the cultural and religious life of the community. In the Christian religion, it is the age for Solemn Communion or Confirmation.

This is not to deny, as we have so repeatedly insisted in the preceding chapter, that childhood is of primary importance in the eyes of any psychologist. But the potential and tendencies of childhood are so numerous and varied and diffuse. It is only in adolescence that they begin to take on a more specific form. In this respect we might well recall an idea that was very dear to Dr. Freud. *A posteriori,* he says, given effect might appear as necessary produced by a given cause; a *priori,* however, it is quite impossible to predict such an effect with any real certitude, particularly an effect of the psychological order, even supposing that we are perfectly familiar with the cause in question. In this principle there is a formal denial of the psychological determinism professed by Freud the doctrinaire — once again in conflict with Freud the man of science. Adolescence is always a time of creation, even though the materials with which it works have been furnished entirely by childhood.

Experience teaches us, moreover, that many psychological traumas occur during adolescence: the most we might reasonably suppose is that a certain predisposition to these particular traumas dates from the time of childhood. On the other hand, I have had opportunity to witness numerous occasions on which the adolescent was able to quite effectively neutralize the traumas of childhood.

Thus we are forced to admit that, from the point of view of mental health, adolescence presents an interest and challenge almost equal to that of early childhood. It is possible to correct against the new mistake to which adolescence itself is always open.

## II. Relationship with Parents

From the beginning of adolescence, the child's relationship with his parents grows considerably more complicated: it is partly for this reason that adolescence is described as an "ungrateful age." Even supposing that no new problem enters into the picture to vitiate this relationship, the four or five years over which adolescence normally extends are generally just barely enough time to bring this relationship back to normal. If the situation is handled awkwardly, there is some danger that a normal relationship will never again be reached, and the individual's whole life can be seriously handicapped as a result.

Up to the age of adolescence, despite his little evidences of self-will and his gropings toward autonomy, the child still showed an obvious preference for the feeling of security he enjoyed with his parents. His parents were more or less the incarnation of his ideals; they were the primary, if not the only, object of his love. The little girl kept saying that she wanted to marry her daddy, and the little boy wanted to have his mother for a wife — and this can be perfectly well understood without having recourse to the famous Oedipus complex.

In adolescence, this circle of intimacy, his whole system of emotional securities is violently shaken. The adolescent has become more conscious, often exaggeratedly so, of his own personality, and he wants more than anything else to be himself. With this in mind, he begins to cultivate his own originality, and frequently likes to think that he cannot become a real man (or a real woman) unless he breaks his bonds with childhood.

The young person no longer finds his parents in such perfect harmony with his ideal. He looks at them in a more objective and even critical light, sometimes with open malevolence. In discovering their numerous defects, he is both pleased and disappointed. He is pleased because their defects give him a legitimate reason for his desire to be emancipated. But at the same time he is sad to see his old idols tumble. It is, perhaps, in an effort to soften this sorrowful blow, and at the same time to counteract their feelings of guilt, that so many adolescents like to indulge in make-believe situations in which they see themselves as adopted children or foundlings, or living under some other circumstances in which they are really strangers to their putative parents. Sometimes these "real parents" are characters from a story book, sometimes they are princes or kings, but always they are out of the ordinary. The adolescent feels a certain sense of horror for reality, and still he is making an effort to adapt to this world of reality: it is precisely the difficulties of this adaption which are the unconscious causes of the horror.

We have just alluded to the adolescent's guilt feelings. This feeling is the result of his hostile attitude and reaction towards his parents. In an effort to compensate and satisfy his interior urge to do them justice, to make up for how he feels inside, he will praise them to the sky in front of his classmates and friends, without too much concern as to whether or not his listeners put any stock in his stories about his father's strength or money, and his mother's good looks or accomplishments. He is less concerned in convincing others than in overcoming his own feelings of guilt.

Slow to react to any influence from within the family, the adolescent is, however, very quick to seize upon the least fleeting fancy from outside, and without any appreciable critical spirit at all. This is the age of great enthusiasms: the young man wants to be a teacher, a priest, a movie star. He blindly subscribes to all the opinions of his ideal. Working class families see their daughters turn communist; the children of an atheist embrace some religious faith.

Parents ought not to be particularly disturbed when their adolescent children change their mind so readily. They would have much more reason for concern if these reactions did not take place. That would be evidence of a fixation in an infantile stage. Particularly, they ought never to lead their children by force or by indirection along "the right path," that is, reduce them to a state of docility proper only to a small child. Christian parents need not be overly scandalized at the strong sentiments of anti-clericalism or militant atheism that suddenly turn up in their children's thinking. Nor, if the parents are atheists, need they worry about their adolescent children's sudden bursts of religious fervor. These are only normal reactions in a young person who is experiencing the need to assert his independence of thought and feeling. The imminent dialectic of his psyche demands that such self-assertion be made, primarily, at the expense of his *superego,* which is the incarnation of his parents and the time-honored tradition of his sociological environment. The necessary adjustments will generally follow of their own accord, towards the end of adolescence.

### III. The Ambiguity of Reactive Behavior

All this is not to claim that *reactive conversion* in the adolescent is necessarily and always *inauthentic.* Quite the contrary, such changes are frequently a sign that the whole life will be directed along a given path, a choice never to be regretted. But in the normal adolescent, unless there is some clumsy intervention on the part of the parents to vitiate this "conversion," it will gradually, progressively, and as the adolescent grows closer to maturity, begin to lose its negative character, its ingredient of hostility towards the parents, until finally it turns into a positive discovery in the order of personal values.

John, the child of fanatically atheistic school teachers, was converted, at the age of 16, to Catholicism. His attitude towards his parents, to whom he had always been most attached, suddenly became openly hostile: this hostility at first hid behind the guise of "apostolic witness." In the town where his parents where teaching he saw his going to church as a public demonstration of faith. In the young people's clubs he thundered out against the "school without God," and offered all sorts of quite exaggerated examples of the anti-religious propaganda being disseminated there, etc. Although he was a student at the public school, he stood up at a regional meeting to defend the position of the Catholic school. Neither the director of the public schools nor his parents were able to understand John: they were furious with him, and this quite obviously only lent additional fuel to his "fervor." Dismissed from his school and all but disowned by his parents, John liked to think of himself as a martyr for Christ. Fortunately for him, during these trying years of his life, he managed to come into contact with a priest who was both understanding and reasonably well grounded in the fundamentals of psychology.

This priest obviously had a cause to doubt the sincerity of John's conversion to the Catholic faith. For this reason, he helped him to increase the depth of his faith, to bring it into closer harmony with the Gospel. Gradually, and in proportion with this new religious depth, John's hostility towards his family and his social surroundings began to dissolve. A few years later, working as a Catholic priest, he managed to win back the affection of his parents and was on cordial terms not only with them but with a good many of his former schoolmates at the public school as well. He was no longer trying to convert them by force, as had been the case during the years of his first extreme reactions to the faith. His Catholic faith, now that it had lost its fanaticism, was still just as fervent as ever.

Now it is not at all unlikely to say that, if John had not succeeded in finding an intelligent priest to guide him, he would never have become a priest, least of all the very outgoing priest that he is today: he might very well have ended up in a mental hospital. In order to escape the threat of schizophrenia, towards which, to judge from the evidence, he seemed to be inclined, it was absolutely necessary for him to be reconciled with himself and with his parents, who are, after all, only a sort of prolongation of his own ego.

## IV. *Love and Trust*

The adolescent, just like the child, needs to know that he is loved. Despite his bravado and his air of self-assurance, he is, actually, very unsure of himself, the outside world towards which he tends with all his youthful energy appears to hold as much threat as it does promise. Still the parental affection that he needs at this age must be expressed much differently than in the love and tenderness that is extended to the very young child. To begin with, it must be very discreet.

Parents should meddle as little as possible in his personal affairs, that is, the friendships, social complications, and daydreams of adolescence. The least indiscretion, the least lack of trust in this area could easily give rise to a revolt on the part of the adolescent, or at least, if the child is afraid of open revolt, he will suffer from serious inhibitions and drawbacks along his road to adult maturity. Particularly, parents must never poke fun at their adolescent children's love life: if they do, they might very well take much of the meaning out of what should be the most noble and most natural feeling of any human person. Neither should they heap him with constant advice and insistently counsel him to prudence in this area; love must never be made to appear as something dangerous to young people.

Finally, it does no good to demand to be taken into a son's or daughter's confidence: such confidences are worthwhile only if they are spontaneous, and this spontaneity can only come from harmony of friendly relationship between parents and child, dating from the time of early childhood. But even parents who love their children very wisely should not be particularly alarmed if a son or daughter, who had been accustomed to confide all his secrets to his parents before, suddenly becomes very closemouthed when he reaches adolescence: this is a reaction of the narcissism which is perfectly normal to that period.

There are some "small details" which take on great importance in developing a happy relationship in this respect. For
example, parents must never open their children's letters,
nor even ask to know their contents. The adolescent always
needs to have his little secrets; and if these secrets are not
respected, he will turn hypocrite: he will get letters secretly,
*etc.*

Similarly, it is a mistake to demand too detailed a report
on his whereabouts and activities, and how he spent his money.
The adolescent mentality has something close to an addiction
for being both independent and trusted.

The advice just given to parents is even more valid for any
other person who has to assume the role of educator in dealing
with adolescents. I have been witness to real disasters which
were the results of distrust in the supervision of adolescent
children on the part of the priests and school teachers.

Therese, seventeen, the child of a pious, middleclass family,
joined the communist youth group. She immediately began to
display the extreme of the typical neophyte. She always
volunteered to sell and distribute anti-religious tracts and
propaganda, and she was overzealous in trying to argue
her old neighborhood friends and companions out of their faith.
A few days after joining the Young Communists, she managed
to have a young factory worker as her lover; she wasted no
time in replacing him with another "comrade" who in turn
quickly gave way to a third, and fourth. Sexual promiscuity
and anti-religious fanaticism seemed to be the fundamental
article of Therese's communist Manifesto.

As a result of circumstance which need not be described,
I happened to discover the secret motivation behind this young
girl's behavior. As a student in a school conducted by the
Sisters, she was a very pious and fervent Catholic young lady
and, for this very reason, she was the object of continual
attention on the part of the good Sisters who hoped to see her
enter their community as a nun. Therese herself was not at

all unsympathetic to this idea, and she had often discussed it with her troop chaplain in the girl scouts — she maintained a very open and almost mystical correspondence with this priest, who was a very experienced and outgoing person and in some respects he took the place of Therese's father in the girl's esteem, her father being a very busy businessman and a rather lax Catholic.

One day, by accident, Therese discovered that the letters she received from the priest were regularly opened by the Mother Superior and that some of the letters, those which spoke of religious practices in terms that were not normally used in that particular community, had never been delivered to her. The result was a violent revolt on her part, a "loss of faith," joining the Young Communists, a conduct that was both provoking and contrary to everything the Sisters had taught her.

The reactions of all young people are, fortunately enough, not so extreme as those just described. Still I could cite a number of cases in which indiscretion or lack of trust on the part of Christian educators has led to very unfortunate results. It is better to face the risk of having a confidence abused, seeing freedom poorly and unwisely used, than to provoke a revolt by refusing to offer freedom and confidence. Even the trials a parent or educator might experience in having to face a whole series of abuses still do not justify the extreme expedient of taking back the trust and confidence that have been offered. There is a profound psychological trust in the advice Mahatma Ghandi gave to his disciples: Trust your fellow man despite his obvious evidences of ill faith. He will deceive you one time, two times, ten times, but finally your trust in him will triumph over his bad faith and he will want to show that he deserves it. We might think that, in our civilization, such advice is hard to apply, and too risky, in the political and social sphere. But as far as mental hygiene is concerned, it is very sound advice and certain to be effective in almost every case.

## V. Aggressiveness

The various problems discussed above show that aggressiveness occupies an important place in the adolescent psyche. It is not restricted merely to family relations. The adolescent proves to be destructive, quarrelsome, excessively intolerant; he is provocative both in his language and in the way he dresses and behaves.

Understanding parents and educators systematically avoid the combats which the adolescent constantly attempts to provoke. What is more, they must avoid such situations without the least sign of disdain or superiority. The adolescent likes to test his strength: he acts as if he were already an adult. Still his unconscious mind is well aware of the fact that he is not yet an adult and that his weakness is still greater than his strength. Thus he must never be told: "You can't understand this yet, these things are beyond your grasp." At this time of life the adolescent is faced with a great temptation to feel misunderstood and even persecuted. Even more so than small children, adolescents must always be taken seriously: irony and sarcasm are harmless only among adults. Young people are too tragically caught up in this struggle with the problems and mysteries of existence to be capable of mere dilettantism, even (and particularly) when they try to sound skeptical of blasé.

As for the adolescent's lack of ideological tolerance, there is generally a way to keep from arguing with him, without making it look like an insult on the part of the adult. The worst problem here is the fact that far too often parents and teachers themselves are not quite grown up enough. They let themselves be drawn into discussions which can easily force the adolescent into taking a rebellious position and conducting the argument in terms that are necessarily excessive and provocative.

But while refusing to be led into any heated debates, adults must still be willing to have serious discussions with the adolescent, "man to man" (or "woman to woman") talks, on any of the subjects which happen to interest them. They never hide behind their prestige as "grown-ups" in an effort to force the authority of their own point of view on the adolescent. The adolescent has a horror of authoritarianism: he wants to be convinced, not told.

It is moreover quite necessary to know that excessive aggressiveness, at this age, is far less serious than its absence. In the first case, parents and teachers can hope that, gradually, as the adolescent matures intellectually and emotionally, the rough edges will be smoothed off. But in the second case, there are grounds to fear that the young person in question will never turn into an "ego," never be self-sufficient, that he will be incapable of facing the struggles and competition of life.

## VI. Narcissism

A more or less extended period of narcissism seems inevitable during adolescence. The young man or lady feels misunderstood by his family, because they keep right on treating him like a child when *he feels* that he is an adult. Often he likes to imagine that he is superior to those around him, because he judges himself according to the nobility and grandeur of his aspirations and ideals, while he measures others on the basis of what they have actually accomplished. He is always tempted to shut himself up behind a haughty front of isolation, in a romantic interior monologue.

This inclination, natural though it is, can take a heavy toll on the adolescent psyche, especially when the child has previously grown up within a very narrow family circle, in the case of a "mama's boy" or "papa's girl" — often in the case of only children. If they are not helped to find a speedy solution to their narcissistic universe, there is every indication that, before they reach the age of twenty, they will have withdrawn into a neurotic condition. This condition, as we have explained elsewhere, *The Depths of the Soul,* chapters 10 and 11, most frequently results from the fact that the emotional energy, the famous *libido,* has never been put to use in a more positively creative direction.

Obviously the best natural antidote for juvenile narcissism is to be found in the child's natural instinct towards companionship, a feeling which is particularly active during these years. Parents must come to understand that even the worst companions are less dangerous for their adolescent youngster than isolation within the "warm intimacy of the family." From a psychologist's point of view, there is only good to be predicted from the fact that fewer and fewer children are being forced to do their learning at home. School is the best place for the child to learn how to live in society: it is an indispensable step towards normal extroversion.

When she was a very young child, Joan was always very clumsy and shy and easily frightened unless she was with her mother. Her mother, disappointed in her marriage, had only one goal in life: to dedicate herself wholly to her daughter. She never let the girl do any of the work around the house, nor show any other signs of initiative. Through the aid of correspondence courses, she personally saw to her daughter's education, up to the age of fifteen. It is no wonder that, under conditions such as these, when Joan was sent to a secondary school for further education, she was a "loner," forming no ties with any group and almost always very homesick for her mother. At the age of nineteen she was seriously sick and needed a long and expensive treatment at the hands of a psychiatrist. The mother couldn't understand why her daughter should hate her so thoroughly and try to avoid her company as much as possible. After all, didn't she do everything humanly possible to spare her daughter's tender sensibilities from the shocks and turmoil of society and contact with a hostile environment?

Once again: it would have been a thousand times better for Joan to have faced all these shocks and turmoils and risks, even if it involved a great deal of unpleasantness. Certainly she would have experienced some difficulty in adapting to the world around her, but more likely than not she would have succeeded well enough. If, at the age of puberty, she had had the opportunity to transfer some of the affection that her mother enjoyed without rival in her young life, to one of her girl friends or teachers at school, it is quite likely that, at the age of twenty she would not have had such a deep-seated hatred for her mother, but would still love and respect her as a daughter should.

Young people's organizations, such as scouting, seem particularly well equipped to offer the adolescent child precisely what he requires in this respect. Good companionship, plenty of outdoor activity, hero worship, camping, and a love of nature are excellent counterbalances against the narcissistic tendencies of this age. In this respect, it is most unfortunate that scouting does not seem very attractive to young people whose interests are mainly intellectual. Moreover, scout leaders must take pains to see that scouting does not turn into an obstacle along the road from adolescence to maturity, that the more enthusiastic members of their organizations do not turn into perpetual adolescents, as so frequently happens and with such deplorable results. Everything in our experiences leads us to observe that scouting has nothing to offer a young person after the age of 17 except in the case of those who are interested in being scoutmasters and exploring the educational opportunities connected with scouting.

## VII. *Imaginary Stories*

Many adolescents show a marked inclination to lie. No matter how harmful the immediate effects of this habit might appear, it is a mistake to regard them as anything too serious. Most of the time this is another characteristic that goes hand in hand with narcissism and will disappear in its turn. Sometimes, too, the adolescent, and particularly the adolescent girl, finds it difficult to distinguish between the imaginary and the real: girls are inclined to anticipate, in their imagination, what they would like to do or be. Frequently, too, these little lies appear to be the only weapon they have to defend their still somewhat fragile feeling of independence against the indiscretions and overbearing invasions of privacy of which adults are so often guilty in their regard. But by far the biggest number of such adolescent tall tales are the result of pure and simple — and quite harmless — storytelling, without any intention to turn the lie into any personal profit or advantage at all.

Henri, fourteen, the son of middle-class business people, told his best friends at school that he was an adopted child, that he was trying to find his real parents. Each day he invented new chapters in the story of his search. One day he was certain that he was the son of Aga Khan and displayed a letter that he had written to his very wealthy father, proving that he was the long lost son. Next day, he claimed that the answer had come in the mail but his "foster father" had intercepted it and taken it away. A week later, Henri was sure that his parents were somewhere among the banished Russian nobility. His parents eventually began to hear the story and, scandalized by the lies their son was telling, they punished him severely, but without the slightest effects. Finally, acting on a psychologist's advice, they decided to pay no further attention to the matter. Eventually, towards the age of 16, Henri was caught up in some of the more realistic problems of living and stopped making up these fantastic stories all of his own accord.

Marie-France, a child of about the same age, began to invent all sorts of romantic episodes for herself. Her lover was sometimes the family doctor, sometimes the plumber who came to fix the kitchen drain, sometimes the chaplain who accompanied her young people's group on their outings. She regaled her schoolmates and friends with all sorts of very spicy details about the habits and techniques of her imaginary lovers. Obviously, there was not a word of truth in anything she said. The knowledge and spicy details that figured in her stories about her love life were all taken from a little book she discovered in her brother's library. In her case too, the passage from adolescence and its normal tendency towards narcissism was enough to put an end to this storytelling. But, had either Henri or Marie-France been accused of being liars by their parents, or punished for what they said, their adolescent lives, and perhaps their lives as a whole, would certainly have been affected by a persistent narcissism.

The best way to combat this inclination to stretch the truth is the discovery of the causes that lead the adolescent to tell such stories. His secrets and his person must be scrupulously respected; he must be taught to love the real, and he must be made to see the beauty and advantages of the truth. Here once again the behavior of the parents is much more decisive than what they say. Children have an astonishing ability to see through the lies that adults tell: they condemn falsehood in their parents, pitilessly, even though they love to stretch the truth themselves.

Finally, in counteracting these tendencies in the adolescent, it is important not to do any lasting harm to the imagination. This faculty is indispensable to every form of creative activity. In the adolescent, as in the adult, imagination always takes precedence over life. Lack of imagination in a person between fourteen and twenty is an incalculable disaster.

## VIII. The Awakening of Sex in the Adolescent

It is wrong to suppose that the various stages of sexual activity are the only, or for that matter even the principal, criteria for dividing human life into infancy, adolescence, maturity, and old age. It is, however, true that in each of these "ages," sex life has some very specific characteristics, side by side with the other physical and psychic faculties. In the course of adolescence, more than during any other period, sex gives rise to numerous problems whose solution will have a great effect in promoting or inhibiting the general development of the individual. Thus, it is only normal for mental hygiene to be interested in sex in a very special way.

As we have pointed out above, psychological adolescence theoretically coincides with the first physical manifestations of adult sexuality in the adolescent. Still, there are a good many little girls who have their first periods at the age of 10 or 11, well in advance of their "adolescent" years. Others, on the other hand, do not have periods until the age of 17 or even 18, some years after they have already become "young ladies." Also there are some boys who experience an ejaculation towards the end of childhood. Thus there is a certain statistical leeway in equating puberty and adolescence.

On the other hand, it would be a big mistake to look at adolescents as sexually mature. Menstruation and ejaculation are no more than a proof of the physical aptitude for procreation. Psychologically, it takes the whole course of adolescence to prepare a person for the responsible exercise of future sexual activity. Experience has shown that sexual relations, far from helping the adolescent to develop, are a serious traumatic factor in his life. Moreover, the sexual maturity of the child must go hand in hand with his general maturity as a whole and, in our civilization today, this means that it can only develop progressively and gradually.

The adolescent boy or girl, and particularly the girl, is always somewhat embarassed when their parents begin to notice the symptoms of their sexual maturity. The adolescent boy will examine the phenomenon of erection or pubic hair all by himself, or with one or two companions, but will be most scrupulously careful to hide it from his parents, and especially from his mother. The adolescent girl will be all alone, or with one or two of her very best friends, when she examines her developing breasts (or, more rarely, the advent of pubic hair); she is proud of her breasts in front of boys, but does everything she can to hide them from her father, and sometimes even her mother. Intelligent parents will respect this natural shyness: They will not make it an occasion to accuse their adolescent children of being backwards or having no confidence in their parents.

Adolescence is the time of first love. It is true, of course, that the young child's passionate love for the parent of the opposite sex (as we have considered it in the preceding chapter) is also an evidence of love, even if, as in our study, we take exception to the Freudian theory that explains this attachment on the basis of sexual activity. But this infantile love, which does not go beyond the limits of the family circle, is still a narcissistic love. The characteristic future of love in the adolescent is the fact that it breaks the narrow circle of family affections and attaches upon someone outside the family. By this very fact it leads the adolescent outwards, towards a conquest of the outside world, and helps him realize the extroversion that is fundamentally indispensable to his proper development.

In its first manifestations, this extroversion of love is still rather timid. The adolescent's first love is generally directed towards a person who is not too far removed from the family circle, or at least easily identifiable with the parent whom the child loved as a young child. Thus it might be an uncle or an aunt, a close friend of his parents, a teacher .... All this ties in perfectly with the general psychological situation of the adolescent. On the one hand, he needs to be emancipated from his dependence on his parents, but on the other hand, he more or less confusedly realizes that he is not yet able to fly on his own wings. He tends to resolve this ambiguity by beginning to replace his parents' role in his affection by people who still have a strong resemblance to his parents. These first objects of his love are always considerably older than the adolescent himself.

In the second stage of adolescent love, the object of the adolescent's youthful passions will still be a person rather close to the family, but this time someone much closer to the adolescent's age. It will be an older brother's fiancee, a cousin who is just a little older (and vice versa for the adolescent girl). Whereas, in the first stage, the adolescent's love was more or less purely platonic, now certain erotic elements begin to make their presence felt. The adolescent girl will dream of kissing and marriage; the adolescent boy tries to touch — secretly of of course — the body or clothing of the one he loves and, in so doing, experiences an erection. Normally, it is not until the final stage of adolescence that the bond between love and sexual desire is both recognized and accepted for what it is: at first, the young man is much more likely to be embarrassed when he desires the girl he loves.

Under no circumstances must parents, or adults in general, take a light attitude towards these experiences of love in their adolescent children. Notwithstanding his brave airs, the adolescent has very tender sensibilities; he is not very sure of himself, and he is very susceptible to what he hears around him. The mild jokes and half serious remarks that are so common among adults are always poorly understood and can easily have a harmful result on the emotional development of the adolescent. Psychiatrists know that, in the case of very many homosexuals, sexual inversion was at least partially motivated, or promoted, by such unthinking conduct on the part of the parents, obliging the adolescent to inhibit his normal impulses towards persons of the opposite sex.

There is nothing either dangerous or abnormal in these adolescent love affairs, such as described above. It is rather their absence in certain adolescents which ought to disturb parents. Obviously it is not desirable for the passions to be unduly aroused in such premature experiences, for, as we have pointed out above, psychologically, the adolescent is not yet ripe for such experiences. But once again: excepting in very unwholesome neighborhoods it is very rare for the adolescent to carry out his erotic dreams in actual behavior. What is more, persons who have had sexual relations during the time of their adolescence hardly ever have them with companions of their own age, but generally with adults who assume the role of seducer. It is not by fighting against the sex instinct, by forbidding love and making it impossible, that these dangers are best faced, but rather by helping the adolescent sublimate his instinct and his love.

Here we encounter the very delicate problem of the relationship between adolescents of opposite sex. At the risk of shocking the sensibilities and inveterate prejudices that are so prevalent, particularly in Catholic circles of thought, the psychologist has a duty to point out that the advantages of coeducation greatly outweigh its disadvantages. In insisting on the disadvantages, we are closer to the morals and psychology of a bygone era than to our own.

In the days when women had very little to do with the social life of men, when they wanted nothing more than to be schoolteachers or housewives, when a proper young lady would not speak to a young man without lowering her eyes, when innocence and purity were synonyms for ignorance of some of life's most essential problems and areas of experience, at such a time it was obviously not at all desirable for girls to attend the same school as boys. It is true that, even during those days, there was no justification for segregating students from those neighborhoods in which they were permitted to play together after school and frequently formed play groups composed of both boys and girls.

But whatever might have been the reasons for segregation in the days past, in our days separate education of boys and girls has nothing to recommend it at all, no matter what their family or social background. Today, men and women both have access to the same professional activities, claim an equal freedom, and must be equipped to meet on every plane. The supposedly individual education and attention given to some young ladies who are shipped off to "select" private boarding schools is a complete anachronism.

It is moreover quite ineffective, since the young ladies who are so trained are not, by and large, either appreciably "purer" nor particularly better equipped to defend their virtue. One might even go so far as to remark that quite the opposite effects are produced. It is, really, quite difficult not to admit, in the light of experience, that the methods of education which make it their purpose to defend the student against the dangers and seductions of the world are not at all adapted to the conditions of life as it actually exists. What education ought to aim at is the formation of people who are able to stand up against the dangers of life. Purity is a most praiseworthy ideal; it cannot be the fruit of ignorance.

In order to be pure, the relation between the two sexes during adolescence must be simple. In many mixed schools it is customary for boys and the girls to form separate groups during recreation. This is a further concession to the outdated principles that are invoked to justify the concept of segregation in education. According to everything I have been able to observe, the best practice is the one adopted by a number of colleges in the small towns where literary and artistic circles, study groups, and even social groups are allowed to grow up spontaneously, on the basis of natural attractions, among boys and girls alike.

Open companionship between boys and girls, particularly in groups, is obviously the best way to produce really adult men and women, people who are in tune with the conditions of modern living. It is the best antidote not only for narcissism which is a threat to adolescent years but also against the homosexual inclinations which frequently come to light at an age in which the sexual instinct is powerful but still poorly oriented towards its proper object. It is not mere chance that so many young people who are kept within the confines of institutional life still practice masturbation at an age in which the greater number of other adolescents have almost completely overcome this narcissistic stage of sexual pleasure. Nor is it mere chance that most recognized homosexuals owe a large part of their formation to precisely such establishments.

Is there any real grounds to fear that such normal companionship between boys and girls will result in precocious sexual experimentation with the resultant dangers to the girls' virginity? To judge from experience, nothing could be further from the truth. France does not possess any study comparable to the famous *Kinsey Report,* and, I, for my part, find it hard to put too much confidence in such a report. The monograph descriptive method of investigation, such as it is practiced by all psychoanalysts and other psychologists, is, in my judgment, far more reliable and trustworthy.

According to all the information I have been able to accumulate, either directly or through other people, it does not seem that a greater degree of companionship between boys and girls presents any greater degree of danger for the virtue of chastity. As far as boys are concerned, the percentage of those who are virgin when they marry is certainly much higher than it was some thirty or forty years ago. The proportion is unfortunately inverse in the case of young ladies, but there is no statistical evidence to support the theory that the percentage of those who have lost their virginity is any higher in mixed colleges than in institutions where segregation of the sexes is strictly observed — in atmospheres where boys and girls are free to see each other, than in areas where boys and girls do not even dare to be seen together. Quite recently, I had occasion to note that, in a particularly uninhibited surprise party, almost all the young ladies belonged to the private schools in Paris which were the strongest on the principle of keeping the sexes segregated. This fact, of course does not prove anything by itself — excepting perhaps that it is not easy to form a correct judgment on this complex subject.

Still there does seem to be a difference. Among the young ladies who had lost their virginity, the majority of those who were used to an open relationship with young men freely consented to the act, whereas the others, as a general rule, were victims of seduction. On the moral plane, this difference does not have so great an importance, perhaps, but things are quite different on the psychological plane: the victim of seduction hardly ever escapes the effects of a lasting trauma. Those young ladies who, out of religious or social motivation, desire to remain virgins until marriage will succeed much better if they are used to meeting young men: it is knowledge rather than ignorance that gives them the weapons they need.

What is really important is to form men and women who are in a position to face the perils of existence, including the problems that arise from sex. This is obviously much more difficult and demands far more intelligence and skill on the part of the educators than does the alternative of protecting the young people — the protection is generally only an illusion anyhow — against temptations and dangers.

Nor must those adolescents who show no visible interest in the opposite sex be taken for paragons of virtue. Unless they are playing the hypocrite, it is quite possible that they are not particularly interested in their work or school studies either. The normal adolescent ought to have what we generally like to call "problems" of the sexual order: it is the price of growing up.

Friendships between adolescents of the same sex also play a very important part in the process of psychological maturation. Their innate narcissistic nature predisposes the young man or young lady to be more conscious of his own personal authority. But friendships such as this give rise to intense emotional experiences without provoking the feeling of guilt that, in our civilization, far too readily attaches to friendly relationship between persons of opposite sex.

Obviously, this intimacy between boys and between girls does involve some danger of sexual deviation. But still we must not be too concerned with the overadvertised danger of "particular friendships." There are really only a very few cases in which such friendships contain anything contrary to nature, and when there is anything of this kind it is practically always owing to the fact that such friendships are cultivated to the exclusion of all intimacy with the other sex.

In keeping with the narcissistic cast of his personality, the adolescent is almost always alone when he first experiences the pleasure of masturbation. At this age masturbation is almost a general practice, although exceptions are far more numerous than certain doctors and psychoanalysts would have us believe. In the case of the adolescent girl, her sense of shame and propriety is generally more developed than in the case of adolescent boys and she will tend to keep closer check over this instinct — a practice which, moreover, tends to make her look for tenderness rather than pleasure. Still there are many, many young girls who resort to touching themselves for pleasure, frequently under the pretext of personal hygiene. The activity of the superego accounts for the fact that very often adult women have no recollection of such activity at all. And they are in perfectly good faith when they claim they have never practiced masturbation. On the other hand, if it does not seem certain that masturbation is appreciably less popular among adolescent girls than it is among adolescent boys, this is certainly owing, in some measure, to the fact that sexual pleasure in the girl is something far more diffuse and general than in the boy.

It is important to insist on the fact that, in itself and for the vast majority of individuals, masturbation during adolescence presents no danger at all in the physiological or psychological orders. It is a phenomenon which can be considered as statistically "normal" — this means that in Western culture it is found to occur more often than not. It can become really dangerous, however, if the experience of emotional guilt which accompanies it very often should increase in intensity to the level of neurotic guilt. This could arise through fear, which in turn might be the result of ignorance. Neither the emotional guilt which normally accompanies this kind of act, nor the neurotic guilt which can arise, should be confused with guilt in the strict sense. The psychologist always needs to take such facts into account.

Peter, a non-Christian and the son of non-Christians, still masturbated regularly at the age of 30. The act was invariably followed by a feeling of intense agony. He was convinced that he had done something very evil, without being able to explain precisely why masturbation should be an evil at all. He recounted, in the course of psychotherapy, how, at the age of fourteen, he had been caught by his father while he was masturbating. The father, ordinarily a very calm man, had become quite violent and beaten the young boy. He had completely forgotten this event in his conscious mind, but in his unconscious mind, masturbation, evil, and punishment were all bound up together. For years after, the only way he felt upon completing the act he regarded as evil was self-punishment: he would stick himself in the leg with a pin, or deliberately look for some more or less serious business reversals. This naturally enough developed masochistic tendencies in the young man and finally led to neurosis. According to Peter himslf, this was the reason behind his neurosis and such was the general opinion of his doctors. The psychologist first of all had to convince Peter that masturbation did not imply any intrinsic ill will, that in the case of the adolescent it can even be considered as something quite common. Once he was freed from the sense of anxiety, Peter no longer needed to punish himself and very soon he no longer experienced the least desire to masturbate.

In Catholic environments, it is not surprising that masturbation is recognized as a moral problem, whereas in the secular environment the only problem may be considered a psychological one if even that. On the other hand the moral emphasizers, perhaps to counterweigh the secular nonchalance, may overlook the fact that a psychological, or a psychophysical problem is very often involved with roots that may be quite complex while being truly but not so simply explained as being traceable to Original Sin.

This is not to deny that those who train the youngster in the moral aspects of masturbation do not conscientiously try to distinguish what is sin from what is not, but too often along with the moral truth an attitude is conveyed — a moral attitude — which is more neurotically than theologically founded. Because of this attitude, perhaps a complexity of the teacher's own fears, feeling, anxieties, the subject matter of purity, etc. the youngster's sex organs become a center of additional personal conflict. It is not surprising too that this in turn can contribute towards adding weight to normal sexual tension which tends to seek relief through the channels most readily available. The result often is that besides the youngster being morally and factually aware that he has sinned against God's law, he also develops a self-image of being "dirty," worthless, unmanly or what have you. This in turn can have the undesired effect of developing further personal tensions which are so conveniently discharged via masturbation. In such a case a vicious circle develops from which the youngster in time despairs of escaping or even talking about.

The attitude of some priests who have far too little psychology in their training (fortunately the number is growing steadily smaller) only confirms the young man in the conviction that he has now committed the most serious of sins. These priests show no visible sign of reaction at hearing such sins as "not saying morning and evening prayers, disobeying parents, being mean to brother or sister," or lack of charity in general.

The sin of impurity receives almost the total brunt of their questions. The advice then given the young man is frequently quite beyond his capacity to understand and generally of little help in preserving the virtue of purity.

When the adolescent, as is generally the case, falls right back into the same sin, the priest may then consider him as not really trying. In the confessional, the young man will express a firm purpose to sin no more, not to start masturbating again, but this firm intention will generally not survive the first temptation to sin. Embarrassed at having to admit his renewed weakness in front of the priest whom he so admires, or whose remonstrances he fears to hear, the young man is often afraid to confess these relapses into sin: and thus he feels he has committed a sacrilege. In an effort to free himself from such a painful sense of guilt, he easily turns to the most sophisticated line of reasoning to convince himself through the help of an atheistic professor, his reading or his companions — that the Christian religion and the Christian morality are not really true. Very many young men have not so much lost as rejected their religious faith in an effort — generally not conscious — to escape the mental anguish occasioned by these sexual practices. Actually, the mental anguish still persists in the case of very many of these "unbelivers." And since their sense of guilt can no longer be alleviated or obliterated by confession, the threat of a neurotic complication is much more severe.

Very many psychologists think that, thanks to the avenue of religious sublimation, the percentage of young men who practice masturbation is much less among Catholics than it is in other young groups. Among people who no longer acknowledge that masturbation is anything else than a normal legitimate pleasure, there will often literally be no way of knowing its frequency, since it will not be mentioned to priest or psychiatrist. Furthermore, it is possibly true of some cultures, that the more sexually permissive they become, the less masturbation will be practiced by young adults: the reason being that sexual intercourse or homosexual practices take its place.

There are however others who think the opposite — that when Catholics once begin the practice, they generally resort to it more frequently and over a longer period of time than others, due to the concomitant strong sense of anxiety; this anxiety, far from keeping the individual from sin, may very likely contribute to his falling. There is deep psychological truth in the story of the forbidden fruit.

The psychologist, as such, is not competent to decide whether or not masturbation is a sin, nor how serious a sin it is. Psychology is not a substitute for religion or for morality. In its own modest way, psychology can do no more than offer its more precise knowledge of the human soul.

First of all, we should like to remind priests and other guardians of traditional morality that there is no sin unless there is a voluntary act. And in a large proportion of adolescent boys, there is very little that is willful (sometimes no element of will at all) in the impulse that leads to masturbation. In a disturbed adolescent there may be little or no willing involved, and in a healthy normal adolescent, occasionally the impulse may be so strong as to reduce responsibility almost to nil. Considering these factors and considering also the impervious urgency of what appears almost as a biological need at such moments, plus other factors as antecedent and consequent imputability, it is not always so easy to untangle the whole in order to state categorically that a mortal sin has been committed. At the same time, it cannot be denied that all such cases may not be so involved, particularly where the youth admits that he deliberately sought the pleasure offering little if any resistance. All of which adds up to a balance between strictness and license with an understanding not only of moral principles but of human needs, circumstances, and conditions.

Secondly, the advice that is generally given — think of something else, resist the temptation, etc. — is most often quite impractical. Direct resistance of such a temptation, deliberately straining oneself to think of something else may have the boomerang effect of making the temptation more obsessive and irresistible.

It is much wiser to include in our understanding of masturbation what it is in the eyes of every informed psychologist apart from its moral implications, namely, a phenomenon quite in keeping with the narcissism of the adolescent. As we have said above, it generally disappears all by itself when the period of narcissism has passed. If the habit persists, this is a sign of fixation at this narcissistic stage, that is — a leveling-off stage in the emotional development and maturity of the individual. Thus our task is not only — and perhaps, not so much — to struggle against a bad habit but rather in addition to remove the inhibitions that are an obstacle to maturity. Working upon the causes rather than upon the symptoms is, after all, a leitmotif of modern depth psychology.

The first thing to be done in giving effective help to the adolescent is to help him overcome his sense of guilt. But only parents or confessors who are themselves free of all unconscious guilt complexes in this area are capable of giving help. Obviously this does not mean teaching the young people that masturbation is never a sin. Christian morality has no cause to be alarmed at the remedies proposed by depth psychology. Morality is concerned with the free human act, whereas psychology offers remedies against what, in the habit under consideration, has often developed into a determinism in human behavior.

Paul, a 19 year old student, was several times denied absolution in the confessional: the priest felt that he did not have the "firm resolution" to sin no more. It sometimes happened that he would not masturbate for two whole weeks and then, Saturday evening, when he was getting ready to go to confession, the tension became irresistible: as he put it in his own words, "it was stronger than me." The priests with whom he had discussed his problems all reprimanded him for his weakness and lack of will, and as a result the young man began to feel not only that he was an unworthy Christian, but that he was incapable of doing anything worthwhile with his life, that he was condemned to mediocrity and failure. He ran off to a monastery, hoping to shield his weakness from the temptations of the world. But no use: after a few weeks he was back home; he could not remain "pure." Paul was on the threshold of despair, and he entertained thoughts of suicide. It was then that he happened to meet a priest who had some acquaintance with psychoanalysis.

Paul confessed, to this new priest, that he had committed several "solitary sins." To his great surprise, the priest did not even refer to these sins in his questions and exhortation. He insisted more on Paul's proper Christian behavior toward other people. But once again Paul could not keep from masturbating that very night. Confused and humiliated he entered that same priest's confessional on Sunday before Mass. The priest, after a few simple questions realized that the young man was in no need of a second absolution, and insisted that he receive Communion as he was. Evidently the priest, from the answer to his questions, diagnosed a compulsive-obsessional state or a depression of severe proportions. Otherwise he would not have been right to insist that he receive Communion as he was. Through the course of further conversation he was able to convince the young man that he was not committing a sin of impurity unless he gave in voluntarily and freely to the act. "If your temptation comes from dirty books and dirty pictures that you looked at just in order to be sexually excited, then you would be guilty," he told the young man. "But that is not what happens in your case, and still you feel humiliated and miserable."

Little by little, Paul was convinced by the priest and at the same time the priest tried to overcome Paul's excessive narcissism by turning his religious thinking away from the spectacle of his own sins and virtues and orienting him more positively in the field of the apostolate. And little by little he completely lost his annoying habit. No longer sad and discouraged, he turned into an outgoing and active young man.

In my judgment, the real cause of persistent masturbation is often some form of narcissism, and it is only by working against this narcissism that the adolescent can be helped to overcome his habits. Discovering the world of other people, learning to have a taste for activity — that is what is needed to fight effectively against "solitary sin." The energy that is held in check by this "bad habit" needs to be directed toward a more positive goal. Whereas the constant inhibition of this energy under the direction of moral precepts can easily create the condition that predisposes a person to neurosis; sublimation of the same energy does much to promote the normal emotional development of the adolescent.

## IX. Sex Education and the Education of the Emotions.

Many parents and educators look upon our modern concept of sex education as an almost universal panacea for all the dangers that threaten the development of the personality through the crucial period of adolescence. It is certainly true that the complete ignorance of sexual matter in which young ladies used to be kept, under the guise of preserving their "innocence" — and this up to the very day of their marriage — has produced an incalculable evil from which our generation, no matter how emancipated it is in other respects, can never be wholly free.

We have said above that, in the case of the girl, the central event of adolescence, both on the physiological as well as the psychological plane, is the onset of menstruation. In many cases this leads to a real psychic trauma. To understand how a natural physiological process can give rise to such unfortunate effects, we must examine the ancient customs and prejudices which are shared by many peoples.

In almost every poorly developed civilization menstruation is considered as something impure. In the Old Testament, as in many other ancient bodies of law, there were severe restrictions against having sexual relationships during menstrual periods, in some cases punishable by death. In our civilization, fortunately, such severity is no longer the rule, notwithstanding the fact that only a very few families regard menstruation as a simply physiological phenomenon. Still, there are not many young girls whose mothers manage to offer a satisfactory explanation of this subject and thus help them overcome their tensions and fears. The girls notice that their mothers and older sisters periodically suffer from some mysterious pain that embarrasses them and which they try to hide. Their older companions explained the process, in their own unsatisfactory way. The result is always a very strong curiosity, in the pre-adolescent girl, a curiosity which very easily passes over into anxiety when the mysterious pain begins to concern them personally.

The best solution, obviously, is for mothers to undertake their children's sex education (for want of a better word) themselves, gradually and progressively. This is particularly important in the case of girls, since, as we have just seen, for them puberty is a far more disturbing experience than it is in boys. A young girl of 11 or 12 ought to be perfectly resigned to the concept of sex in general and her own sex life in particular.

Obviously, it is quite proper to have a collective initiation to the question of sex at school. But, in order to be in any way useful and not have any traumatic effects on some of the more sensitive children, such an initiation must necessarily remain on the level of mere teaching. Here more than anywhere else, teaching cannot be identified with education. Teaching on the subject of sex, such as it can be offered in the school, must necessarily be limited to the biological and physiological aspects of the question. As for its personal aspects, those aspects which touch most profoundly on the emotional development of the child, it can only be explained on an individual basis, by someone who knows the child much more closely, someone who is aware of his maturity level and its psychological implications.

No matter how earnest our desire to "demystify" sexuality for the child, only a total ignorance of the complexity of the problem could lead us to believe that it can be taught with the same scientific objectivity as, for example, the other bodily functions, such as digestion and respiration. This might not be as we want it to be, but how can we escape the fact that everything that is connected with sex is necessarily and profoundly veiled in mystery. There is always serious danger in doing away with a mystery that is so profoundly anchored in the collective unconscious of humanity: all we should attempt is to shed a little more light on it. As experience has shown, so-called sex education is really the beginning of many painful traumas in countries where it is generally taught collectively in the classroom.

In order to do a good job in such a delicate area of education, it is most important for mothers themselves to be completely free of any unconscious feeling of guilt in this area.

Still, no matter how indispensable this sex education appears to be, that is, the practice of supplying adolescents with these theoretical notions about sex, it would be a serious mistake to regard this as a solution to the essential problems of adolescence. We must not ever lose sight of the fact that sex is only a part — a most important part to be sure — of the total emotional life. It is the education of the emotional life as a whole to which the process of education must be addressed if it is to offer any real help to the problems of adolescence. Sex education can give the desired result only if it is conceived and practiced as one chapter in the over-all emotional education as a whole. Otherwise, there is always the danger of doing more harm than good, if only by giving the adolescent an impression that sex is the pivotal point of his existence.

# PART II

# MENTAL HYGIENE AND THE ADULT MIND

# 4 the body-soul equilibrium

Together with the majority of psychologists and psycho-therapists, we have discovered from experience that it is primarily during the formative years of childhood and adolescence that mental health is most seriously threatened. The structures of the ego are more fragile then, and shock and frustration have much farther-reaching repercussions. Once mental hygiene and sound psychology have managed to preserve the mind from trauma up to the age of 17 or 18, then, theoretically, psychic health can be considered as all but definitively established.

But unfortunately, mental hygiene is in a position — in its present state of development and surely for a good many years to come — only to diminish the threat of trauma. As we have stressed in the introduction, the fundamental principles of this science are far less observable and far less developed than those of bodily hygiene and we all realize that bodily hygiene is unable to preserve humanity from every epidemic and every disease.

## I. The Danger of Neurosis in the Adult

The effect of the shocks and frustrations undergone in childhood and adolescence do not always show up at once. It is not at all rare for an individual who had an extremely disturbed childhood and adolescence to show no visible signs of psychic disorder for a good many years. This is because the conditions of his existence are favorable and afford him enough happiness and scope for development to effect an almost complete neutralization of the evil effects of the traumatic shocks he has experienced. We must not consider such a person as immunized, however: the neutralizing of these traumatic shocks does not actually remove the trauma itself. All that it takes is a shocking experience at an adult age, or even in old age, and for that matter a shock that is not objectively violent, and the neurosis will manifest itself, generally to the complete surprise of the subject and his circle of acquaintances.

During fifteen years of married life, Renee passed for a perfectly happy woman in the eyes of all her acquaintances and friends. Only her husband knew how excessive a need for tenderness and affection she had. She could not, for example, fall alseep at night except in her husband's arms, her head pillowed on his shoulder. But even he considered this as nothing more than an evidence of her love for him.

One day, Renee happened to see her husband engaged in cheerful and animated conversation with one of her best friends. She experienced a twinge of jealousy at once, but hardly thought it significant: she told herself that obviously there was nothing wrong or suspicious in such a conversation. But still, from that moment, her conduct became more and more puzzling. She could no longer stand their apartment: they moved and she was no more content with their new quarters. Every night she would wake up several times with a start, convinced that she had forgotten to turn off the gas; she had to go out to the kitchen and check each time, and she was always completely astonished to discover the gas turned off sight. A few hours later she would be certain that she had opened it when she was checking it the time before, and would have to go back again, to check once more. Whenever her husband or children were even the least little bit late, she began to imagine that all sorts of terrible accidents had occurred: she would tremble, break out in a cold sweat, and her teeth would chatter. Despite the fact that her fears were never borne out by reality, she was always perfectly convinced that each new presentiment of evil was about to materialize.

In the course of psychotherapy it came out that in her early adolescence Renee had suffered a good deal from the deep misunderstanding between her parents whose divorce, when she was only 13, had put her in a terrible state of mental confusion, since she could not decide which of her parents she wanted to live with. Her natural preferences ran towards her father, because she considered him more necesssary than her mother. This anxiety was soon aggravated by a most shocking incident: a friend of her mother's new husband made improper advances upon her, and she was very disturbed by this incident for several months.

Then, from her fifteenth year onward, Renee's life became so intense and happy that she had completely forgotten the unfortunate experiences of her childhood. Her brilliant scholastic record and the nineteen years of marriage with a good husband whose calm reassurances gave her the perfect security she craved had managed to neutralize the traumas of her adolescence. Theoretically, this state of affairs could have lasted to the end of her life. But as it turned out, an event that was very insignificant in itself, coinciding with her menstrual period (which always made her hypersensitive), was enough to break down all the defenses that had protected her against neurosis.

Renee's case is a good example of the fact that so-called preventive medicine against neurosis, mental hygiene, needs to continue far beyond childhood and adolescence. Much more than bodily health, it is practically indispensable all throughout a person's life. In the case of young people, its purpose is to keep them from traumatic experience: for adults, it is needed to keep the traumas of the past from breaking out into neurotic patterns of behavior. One other obvious difference between the two stages of mental health is the fact that during childhood and adolescence it is up to parents and teachers to apply the proper techniques and safeguards: the adult has to see to this himself.

Sensitive persons, if they are aware of having had a sad or broken childhood, must take proportionately more care than others in seeing to their psychic equilibrium: unfortunately it is precisely such persons who find it harder to concentrate on psychic health because of the fears they already have. All too easily they manage to convince themselves that everything is going well and they are far too willing to forget the troubles of years gone by.

But even those who consider themselves strong and well balanced, and rightly so, would do well to respect the elementary principles of mental hygiene. No one is ever in a position to swear that he is completely exempt from the danger of neurosis, that his unconscious is not at grips with any unresolved conflicts. It goes without saying that mental hygiene must not be a sort of obsession, that it must always remain within the limits of the normal sensible precautions that are suggested.

On the other hand, we know too that no amount of hygiene is going to absolutely and unconditionally guarantee the health and equilibrium of body or soul. No matter what precautions we take, surprises are always possible, if only in the form of shock too violent for our defenses to cope with. But we have already accomplished very much if, thanks to the insights of mental hygiene, we have managed to immunize ourselves against the more habitual shocks that affect our daily living, if we have reduced the element of risk.

## II. Mens Sana in Corpore Sano — Healthy Mind in a Healthy Body

This famous maxim of Juvenal is always applicable. Not too many years ago, it was customary for a young "intellectual" to scoff at hunger and eating, to be ashamed of having muscles or a broad chest. Fortunately, we have passed beyond that stage today. Even the snobs of our day no longer act as if bodily health were an obstacle to the fuller activity of the mind. Even the masters of Christian asceticism are beginning to admit that it is perhaps not absolutely indispensable to reduce the body to a state of slavery in order to enjoy an intense spiritual life. Thanks to the spectacular progress of depth psychology, they realize that a slave, even the human body when it is reduced to an absolute slavery, tends to exert all its efforts to break the chains that are forged to hold it captive. Nothing is more negative or destructive than an insurrection of enslaved power.

Our whole effort must be directed towards a harmonious coexistence between flesh and spirit. The opposition that some writers like to stress between these two components of our human nature is certainly not Christian in Inspiration. St. Augustine and St. Thomas Aquinas teach nothing on this subject that is at variance with the findings of modern psychology.

Henri Bergson sees lack of equilibrium between material growth and spiritual growth in the world of today as the principal source of the disorders and misery of which we are victims. Whether the subject under discussion is individual or collective existence, it is hard not to be struck by the element of extreme fragility. Societies, the British Empire for instance, which but a short time ago seemed possessed of an unshakable solidarity, are now declining and disintegrating with alarming speed. Family circles built up on the most sublime conjugal ideals dissolve before our very eyes for reasons that are obviously not well founded. Men and women of fervent faith and proven morals, firmly rooted in the best traditions and principles, show themselves capable of the worst folly: at the drop of a hat they betray everything that seemed to be the very substance of their being.

Andre, the son of a rich and noble family, was a brilliant naval officer. He was making his way in the world very successfully, engaged to a young lady who was a perfect match for him in every way. At the age of 27, under the activity of divine grace, but without any of the elements of a spectacular conversion — for he had always been a fervent Christian — the young officer abandoned his career, his fortune, and his love to enter a religious order. After a period of intense spiritual and intellectual formation, he was ordained a priest. His radiance and influence were remarkable; he was quickly set up as an example to the novices in the order. Then, all of a sudden, the whole monastery was shocked to hear that this very exceptional priest had abandoned his priesthood and married a barmaid who was entirely without education or breeding.

Such a case obviously involves some element of psychopathology. If it were only an isolated example, it would be wrong to treat the subject at any great length. But unfortunately, it is only one from many similar examples: it seems that the number of men and women who are capable of making such an incomprehensible (logically incomprehensible, that is) rejection of all good sense and their own most cherished principles has become legion. There is no grounds for fearing the imminent destruction of our planet and of all mankind by the gradual cooling off or heating up of the solar system or some other cosmic catastrophe: today there is more and more evidence of the fact that it is the stupidity of men themselves that constitutes the gravest threat to our individual and collective future.

### III. Neurosis as a Danger in Society

For a long time psychoanalysis has been interested only with the individual. But little by little it has been led to recognize the fact that, on its own specific terrain, the individual, isolated, is no more than an abstraction. Whenever we try to make a concrete reality out of this abstraction, we run headlong into the wall of reality, and our chances of coming off unharmed are not always good.

In order to be "normal" and healthy, a man must recognize that he is, and must want to be, a member of the community, or rather a member of a great number of communities. It is the mission and duty of mental hygiene not only to make him realize and accept this necessity, but to help him make a solid place for himself in the different communities to which he belongs by his position in life, without letting him run the risk of being refused by the community or of introducing some element of disorder into the community to which he already belongs. On the other hand, mental hygiene ought to help us belong to those communities we need in order to prevent a deterioration of our own individuality.

Mrs. F., who appeared to be normal and outgoing, was, because of her many unconscious conflicts, so extremely aggressive that other people were almost always annoyed and upset when they had to deal with her. Because of her unconscious inferiority complex, she mistrusted, *a priori*, everyone she had to deal with: she criticized and attacked them, frequently without even meeting them halfway. Such behavior of course, led to numerous setbacks in her social relations with these people, and, as a consequence, the shipwreck of all her many plans.

Obviously there can be no question here of radically suppressing every element of aggressiveness. First of all, suppressed aggressiveness is aggressiveness under restraint, aggressiveness which always threatens to react in an even more hostile manner than before. But above all, a certain degree of aggressiveness is natural to the life instinct. It promotes the necessary spirit of competition that life is made up of, and it contributes greatly to success in life. And a man needs to succeed in life, in order to avoid neurosis. Thus the social good does not require the supression of aggressiveness, but rather the conscious integration of its unconscious motivating powers.

### IV. Neurotic Families.

We are indebted primarily to the work of the famous American psychologist, Karen Horney, for our understanding of the fact that the causes of neurosis are not exclusively individual. There are neurotic social environments which are contagious for the individuals who are a part of them. And the family, more than any other community, sets up the most intimate bonds between its members: its influence in neurotic disorders is thus particularly strong.

Too often even the best of psychotherapy fails to accomplish very much for a neurotic patient whose sickness is not particularly serious in itself, simply because the influence of the family atmosphere always counteracts that of the psychologist. Many times it is advisable to treat both husband and wife when one or the other has a serious neurotic problem. It frequently happens that one of the partners was perfectly normal before marriage. But the years of living together with a neurotic person have upset his psychic equilibrium, and now, by his behavior and reactions, it is the formerly sound partner who prevents or retards the recovery of the sick one. It is no paradox at all to say that neurosis is the most contagious of all diseases. Obviously, it is not contagious in the same way that the flu or tuberculosis are contagious: there is no such thing as a neurotic or neurosis microbe: it is rather a question of atmosphere and "wearing off on someone."

In the case of children, it is most difficult, if not absolutely impossible, to prevent them from being contaminated by their neurotic parents. Sometimes in an effort to accomplish favorable results, it is necessary to have them removed from their homes for professional treatment. Such a step does stand a good chance of success, both for the child and the neurotic parent, provided the parent has agreed to submit to psychotherapy. But psychotherapy is largely a waste of time in the atmosphere of family conflict as it actually exists.

Mrs. F. brought her 18 year old daughter to the psychologist because she was abnormally upset and had an "impossibly" bad character. The treatment produced excellent results, but also revealed the fact that the daughter's neurotic behavior patterns were intimately correlated with those of her mother. In order to treat the daughter the doctor also had to treat the mother. But Mrs. F. did not want to admit that she too was a neurotic and she could see no reason for letting the doctor work on her. The psychologist had no other alternative than to suggest, under some pretext or other, that after her treatment was completed, the young lady should pursue her studies in some other city, as far as possible from her mother. This was obviously a most extreme measure; but it was the only effective one.

### V. Neurotic Influences in Modern Living

Our everyday experience shows us that modern social life in itself is most injurious to our psychic balance. Material insecurity, constant hurrying, being uprooted from our surroundings, the constant threat of collective destruction — these are neurotic factors that are at least as dangerous as the individual traumas discussed in the first part of this book. They are even more dangerous, in the sense that the individual is not always in a position to protect himself against them.

The highly praised practice of putting money in the bank,

for instance, used to be considered as a good way to ward off a possible sense of insecurity. But today, those who save their money face perhaps even greater anxiety than those who spend it: the national economy is always threatened by depreciation or economic instability. In certain cases, the psychologist finds himself obliged to advise against putting money in the bank because his patient will find it less a threat to have no possessions at all than to face the constant fear of losing what he has worked so hard to acquire and save.

It would be utopian to want people to stop living in big cities where life is noisy and too hurried and there are no really settled roots. We shall have to be content with those half-measures which will at least partially neutralize the psychic threats of modern living. As far as mental hygiene is concerned the psychologist can only rejoice at the widespread practice of paid vacations which allow almost everyone to escape the noise and bustle of city living for at least a week or two.

Unfortunately some people are so accustomed to this kind of existence that they are no longer able to leave it behind even for a day or two. They are like those neurotics who have lived with their own neurotic conflicts for such a long time that, unconsciously, they set up every possible resistance to their own cure. How many people from Paris, Lyons, or Marseilles leave the noise and bustle of their city life behind them every spring, only to meet the noise and confusion all over again in busy hotels and packed beaches, on the Côte d'Azur, along the Riviera, at Chamonix, with other people from Paris, Lyons, and Marseilles. As far as mental hygiene is concerned, such a vacation is an almost total loss.

A situation such as this is really fashion, or snobbery if you will, influencing good common sense. The widespread practice of camping actually offers a much more peaceful and healthy vacation than the noisy bustle of hotel living. Provided, of course, that the campers do not all flock to the same famous spot, but are content with some quiet little corner by themselves. It is a serious mistake, and an obvious danger to mental equilibrium, to come back from a vacation less rested and relaxed than before the vacation began.

For a vacation, either at some resort hotel or in a tent or under the open sky, to be a proper antidote against the hustle and insecurity of modern living, it would be advisable to spend vacations year after year in the same spot. I have had frequent occasion to substantiate the theory that those who regularly spend their vacations with relatives who lived in the country, even though it was the most unromantic and unpicturesque locality imaginable, and living conditions far from being really comfortable, always found incomparably more balance and relaxation than those who hurried off to a different location each year. The first group felt they were "going back home," that they were wanted and expected: they had roots — and this was obviously not true of the others

This is not to condemn the practice of going on tours. Touring is obviously a very enriching experience and generally offers precisely that element of change in climate and landscape that seems to have become a psychological necessity for so many city dwellers. But only a part of our vacations and a small part at that, should be spent in touring.

There is still a great number (and a growing number) of those who do not feel they are at home in any other town or country. I have often wondered if it would not be wise to persuade such people to leave their homes for a time each year and take up a temporary residence in some of the newer areas that are always being settled and developed.

There are, of course, some families who are well situated enough to own a modest second residence in a little country town somewhere off the beaten path.

Some people are disturbed at the constant decrease in the number of working hours per week, as a result of automation and other fields of technical progress. But anyone who has an eye for the many dangers which our modern way of life and work presents to our collective psychic equilibrium could hardly share such concern. Two months of vacation every year would certainly not be too much to counteract the factors that make for psychic imbalance in the kind of daily life that, by sheer necessity, most people in the larger cities have to lead. Nor is it any answer to say that most people would not know what to do on such a long vacation.

Obviously we cannot expect people who for years have been used to the constant feverish hubbub of city living to find any immediate relaxation in a calm life, with a slower rhythm, in some out of the way little town where "nothing ever happens." But there is every indication that people would get used to it little by little, for their own good and for the good of mankind as a whole. When two weeks vacation first started to be the general rule, there were a good many workingmen who lounged idly around the streets or spent the whole day in the bars and cafes, bored and helpless. But it took no more than twenty years to teach them how to use their new found leisure wisely and profitably.

## VI. The Problems of Specialization

A new factor that contributes to psychic imbalance is the process of specialization as it is being developed and extended and applied to an earlier stage of studies and work. In order to supply the engineers that the country needs so desperately, the trend is to do away with the humanities in education and concentrate on technical preparation. In the United States and in Russia, the process goes even further: even general science studies are pushed into the background in order to concentrate on the immediate preparation of future specialists in chemistry, electronics, radar, surgery, neurology, etc.

Continuing along this line will certainly produce specialists, well trained and effective in the way that robots are effective, but they will be seriously mutilated personalities. It is to be hoped that the progress of technology would permit the abolition of many of the deplorable conditions of manual labor, long recognized as one of the worst results of industrialization. But from the psychologist's point of view, the prospect of a specialized engineer is no more satisfying. This mutilization by "robotization" has a tendency to take hold of every branch of human activity. In many countries a man can become a professor of science without ever having had to take any fundamental courses in general culture first.

How can anyone fail to recognize the fact that excessive specialization, particularly when it begins at such an early age, can only be expected to develop a sort of human monster? Both the intellectual and the physical faculties that the specialist has never needed to use, tend to atrophy, while the hyperactivity of the one faculty he needs and uses only contributes to the general imbalance of his personality.

Still, we are not laboring under any law of necessity here. All it takes is a minimum of intelligent adaptation to the new and changing conditions of life and work, departing from routine and prejudices, and production interests can go hand in hand with the development of our full human personality.

Thanks to the progress of bodily medicine and hygiene, not only is the life span of every man considerably prolonged but a man remains young and vigorous for a much longer time than before. As a result, from the social point of view, retiring a man of 55 or 60, who, for the most part, is still in full possession of both his physical and his psychic powers, is an absurd waste of human resources. As for the men themselves, we shall see, in a later chapter, the evil results of early and prolonged retirement.

By putting off the age of retirement by a few years, it would be just as easy to put off the age at which professional activities begin as well. Instead of lending further momentum to the process of specialization, to the detriment of general culture and development, we might instead not only contain it within its present limits, but actually put it off for a few years longer — thereby taking advantage of the only effective counterbalance to the inevitable advance of specialization in training and industry.

It is harmful for the equilibrium of the individual, and, as a consequence, for the social equilibrium as well, to overload school programs, particularly the schedules of secondary schools, in order to make room for the constantly increasing number of subjects that have to be taught. Secondary education should give everyone a solid grounding in the humanities, a general culture that can develop the human heart and mind. The introduction to specialized studies ought to be confined exclusively to the intermediary cycle between secondary education and higher learning, a cycle that could easily extend over the course of two or three years.

For perfect equilibrium between body and soul, it is indispensable for every manual course to contain a minimum of intellectual education, and for every "intellectual" course to have a minimum of manual training. Every man's field of interests needs to be broader than his particular specialty. Take, for example, a working man who, because of some accident, is unable to go back to his work for several months. If he has no intellectual interests at all, he will necessarily fall prey to a terrible feeling of boredom, unable to occupy his leisure time to any advantage. Such is the sad lot not only of manual laborers as such, but also of many others whom we generally call "men of action" — businessmen, industrial men, etc. I have known men who have undergone a severe depressive crisis following a very brief period of forced inactivity. The same thing is true of many career women, and socialites, once they no longer have their busy social calendar to fill their time.

On the other hand, too many intellectuals are lost as soon as they are separated from their books. And only a very few are able to spend every day of the year and every hour of the day on their books without the risk of serious mental harm. Unfortunately too many intellectuals do not know how to occupy their days off and their idle moments: there is often far too much intellectual activity in homes where time would be better spent in less demanding forms of relaxation.

Mental hygiene considers hobbies and side interests as something very important for every individual. And their subject matter should be as far removed as possible from the individual's professional activity. The business man who has a passion for painting or poetry, the philosophy professor who is a judo amateur, the housewife who belongs to a literary circle or a bowling team — such people have a considerably better chance of safeguarding the youth and health of their minds.

## VII. Over-activity

In many social circles and in many professions, overdoing has become such a current phenomenon that some people openly boast about how much they do, even though in reality they have very little to be proud of. Students and professors, intellectuals as well as workingmen, mothers as well as business women — all alike complain of their chronic tiredness and fatigue. Their taste for life is at low ebb and their work is far less effective than it should be. Often, such a condition leads to a very painful state of anxiety or depression.

Yet it seems that, in most cases, it is not so much an excessive work schedule that exhausts them as it is their inability to pace themselves. The mind needs relaxation as much as the body does, and this relaxation should be as complete as possible. Rather than lack of time, it is more often a simple lack of skill that makes proper scheduling difficult if not impossible.

Michael was an engineer in an important laboratory. He

felt that he was never doing enough during the daytime: he brought blueprints and designs home with him, and worked on them until late into the night. When he was asleep, he even dreamed of his work. He had no time left to take an interest in his wife and children; he had no interests outside his work. Contrary to what might generally be believed, this over-dedication to his work contributed nothing towards increasing his effectiveness. Quite the contrary, in his laboratory he set to work without very much enthusiasm; he complained of an almost constant state of fatigue and found it all but impossible to keep his mind on what he was doing.

A psychologist he consulted advised him to never bring his professional work home, under any circumstances, to take up golf or tennis or join a club, and to always devote a part of his evening leisure to conversation with his wife about the children's school work. He was further advised to spend all day Sunday out in the open, not reading any of his technical work, but playing with his children as much as he could, walking, getting exercise. Michael followed the doctor's advice and, at the end of three months his depression and anxiety had completely disappeared. His work at the laboratory noticeably improved, to the point where he no longer needed to carry a brief case home at all, even if he wanted to. His married life also profited immensely from the new sense of organization.

Elaine and Joan were two young married women: they had studied at the same universities and belonged to the same social class and had the same number of children. Neither of them had any outside help around the house. Joan was never finished with her housework or her children, never had a single free minute for reading or listening to music or serious conversation: she was always busy picking something up or getting something ready. Elaine, on the other hand, managed to find some few free hours every day to lose herself in philosophical or theological or literary activities. What is even more remarkable is the fact that it was her house, and her children, that were the clean and tidy ones, not Joan's.

In my own experience I have frequently noticed that whenever I managed to tear away from my work and spend a few days in a tent somewhere (without books or paper or even a pencil), I have always noticed an improvement, both in quality and quantity, in my intellectual stamina and output when I returned.

The results produced by our work depend much more on the intensity than on the duration of our efforts. "Intense living" might well be a sort of catchword for mental hygiene. Experience proves that it is not possible to live intensely if we have not learned how to separate the hours of work and the hours of leisure, assigning each one its proper time and activities. Together with a good many educators, I am firmly convinced that if homework were done away with our students would work much harder at school. As things are right now, they have practically no interruption in their scholastic activity; in fact many children are still working on their problems and compositions when they have fallen asleep at night. They even dream of their school work. Under such conditions, it is no wonder that the results are so discouraging.

The frantic rhythm of life as it is lived today, the monotony of so many professional duties, even in the so-called intellectual pursuits, makes it absolutely imperative to have a division of time between work and leisure. It is for want of this sensible element of leisurely relaxation in their daily living that so many people have recourse to the pseudo-relaxation offered by alcohol, tobacco, and sedatives.

Another trend that needs to be resisted as strenuously as possible is the increasing standardization of human beings. This is not a question of promoting personal individuality; communication with other people and belonging to the community are more indispensable than ever to personal equilibrium. But only a man who is really himself can face the demands of life and make a worthwhile contribution to the community. Relations between people must not ever be set up along the lines that operate in the anthill or beehive: they must always be inter-personal.

# 5 sex problems

Like every other non-Freudian psychologist who takes up the discussion of problems relating to sex, we find ourselves in a paradoxical situation.  On the one hand, we frequently criticize the excessive importance accorded to the problem in Freud's psychology, and on the other hand in each chapter of this book we do have a lot to say about this same problem, and now we are about to devote a rather lengthy chapter precisely to that subject.  But the paradox is only in appearances.  In refusing to accept the pan-sexualistic dogmatism of Freud, we never intended to lose sight of or minimize the very important role that sex has to play in every phase of our existence.

## I. Neurosis and Sex

Neither clinical observation of the facts nor philosophical reflection gives any basis for the claim that the root of all psychic conflict is to be found in unconscious sexual conflict, nor the fact that all human activity is conditioned, or even determined, by the transformation of the sexual libido.

On the plane of psychological practice, I myself generally avoid taking the initiative in any discussion of sexual problems, if only because of the fact that the vast majority of patients who consult a psychologist are convinced that this will be the only area the doctor wants to discuss. Discretion on the part of the psychologist thus almost always has a very salutary effect. It makes the patient much less nervous. The patient had formed a mental picture of what to expect, and, obviously embarrassed at having to discuss such areas of experience with someone he does not yet know, he has prepared a partial and highly colored version of his problems. When the psychologist actually begins the discussion by speaking about other matters, the patient is at first pleasantly surprised, and then much more at his ease. By the fifth or sixth visit, almost every patient comes out with his problems in this area all by himself, quite spontaneously, without being asked. And very, very rare is the neurotic patient who does not have some difficulties in this area. And since, by that time, the psychologist is no longer a stranger, the patient feels much freer in discussing it.

Frequent as sexual problems are in the neurotic patient, they still do not appear to be the fundamental psychic conflict. The relative frequency of such problems seems rather due to the fact that most adults today have had no emotional or sex education. As a result, an instinct as strong as sex almost completely escapes their conscious control, and seems to be abandoned to the anarchy that is characteristic of all instinctive impulses. The great progress that has been made in the sex education of children permits us to hope that future generations will see a much smaller number of people who are sexually handicapped. But it is still true that, for men and women as they are today, and for adolescents, too, the psychology of mental hygiene will have to leave an important place for the consideration of problems that are directly or indirectly related to sex.

What is more, no matter how serious the errors and short-comings of education, there is no reason why neurosis should be the necessary result. Frequently enough, the real cause of neurosis are other unresolved psychic conflicts — the sexual conflicts being only an annoying syndrome.

We have seen that neurosis can break out at any age, even though it is true that the initial trauma generally dates back to childhood or early adolescence. Psychic hygiene, in the adult, is aimed at preventing the latent trauma from coming out into the open. In the preceding chapter, we reviewed the most important techniques for achieving this end. But, since the problem of sex usually takes on a more personal and individual importance, it deserves a complete chapter.

## II. Chastity a Danger?

The sex instinct is one of the most powerful human instincts, if not the most powerful. Like every other instinct, it is meant to serve some fundamental need. The satisfaction of this natural need makes it possible to discharge the psychic tension that rises from this instinct. Normally, sexual satisfaction among adults takes the form of sexual intercourse.

Many virtuous persons and even some well intentioned moral teachers have turned sex into the pivotal point of a religious and moral life, subconsciously, defining vice and virtue with reference to sex and purity. And thus, quite contrary to their intentions, they give substance to even the most excessive Freudian theses of Pan-sexualism. At the risk of scandalizing some pious people, the psychologist must recall that, in itself, sexual continence is not a virtue, that virginity — always "in itself" once again — is not necessarily a particularly good thing, any more than the Christian virtue of abstaining from alcoholic liquor or Friday abstinence. It is true that, from a rigorously natural point of view, drunkenness and dissipation are harmful and ugly, and as such they are reprehensible. But normal modern habits of eating and drinking and sexual pleasure really have nothing in common with these abuses.

Chastity, just like fasting and abstinence, can turn into a virtue, that is, something morally worthwhile, only when a man chooses it freely and for a higher motive which is objectively good. The same thing is true of the young lady who renounces marriage because, for example, her aging father needs her help. The same is true of the young man who is preparing to enter the priesthood in a church which, for reasons of which she alone is the judge, requires celibacy in her ministers. It goes without saying, however, that those who find themselves obliged to observe celibacy and chastity despite themselves, can always turn the force of necessity into a trans-valuation of what is in itself only a painful restriction of their human freedom.

Theoretically, every human being has a right to sexual satisfaction, just as he has a right to food and drink. But it is a mistake to push this analogy between the various human instincts too far. Hunger and thirst are only incidentally concerned with human freedom: they have to be satisfied or else the individual will perish. Notwithstanding the contrary protestations of a certain libertinism which is growing slightly out of fashion today, the same is certainly not true of the sex impulse. In many circumstances its immediate satisfaction can, from the point of view of mental hygiene, lead to consequences which are very harmful both for the individual and for society.

Thus we know that both man and woman are physiologically developed enough for sexual activity from the onset of puberty. In the case of certain adolescents, the impulses of the sex instinct are very imperious even at this age. But it remains true that, as a general rule, precocious sexual relations, far from promoting the proper development of the person, always lead to very unfortunate consequences and threaten to retard the complete maturation of the individual and his psychic equilibrium.

This apparent paradox is explained by the fact that the sexual instinct, more than any other instinct, goes far beyond the merely biological element and strikes its roots deep within the human psyche. Now it is one and the same emotional energy which feeds all our psychic energies. The young person needs a good deal of this psychic energy for the development of all his faculties, both intellectual and emotional, and for his general adaptation to life. If a noteworthy part of this energy is already oriented towards sex activity,* this can only redound to the detriment of his psychic totality.

These facts might well lead us to conclude that, from the individual point of view alone, chastity is a practical necessity until the end of adolescence. As far as procreation is concerned, the social function of sex, it has often been proved that excessive youth in parents is just as harmful and undesirable as excessive old age. This subject will come up once again, but we have already said enough to show that concerted intervention of the Church and public morals and education is well justified in an effort to oblige people to restrain their sex impulses. We must however recall what we discussed in the chapter on adolescence, namely that this intervention must be positive and never take on the *superego's* character of force or constraint.

Because of their misunderstanding of Freudian theories, many people still think that chastity, if not radically impossible, is at least extremely harmful to both physical and psychic health. There are still some doctors and psychologists (fewer, fortunately, than there were twenty years ago) who recommend adultery or a regular visit to the brothel for all their neurotic patients who complain of any anxieties or obsession. The actual problems such people suffer are really much more complicated.

We have just said that the sexual function is unquestionably the greatest consumer of affective energy. The more libido a man has, the greater his sexual drives. Obviously it

---

* Cf. *The Depths of the Soul, Ch. IV.*

would be dangerous to leave such a dynamo of energy unused. It would almost certainly manage to break the dikes reared to contain it and burst out lawlessly in all directions. Obsessions, hallucinations, perversion, the most shameful crimes — these are frequently the result of overrestraining the libido. Public opinion some years ago was quite shocked to hear of the terrible crime of a humble country priest who killed his mistress and the baby she was expecting. Some people tried to turn this into an argument against clerical celibacy. Actually it is an argument only against a purely negative form of that celibacy. It is very dangerous and morally evil to forbid the use of sex and its release of psychic energy without also being sure that there is some other outlet for that energy.

Mental hygiene sees nothing commendable in the concept of negative chastity such as it is forced upon the inmates of prisons and other institutions of a like nature. On the other hand, there is nothing objectionable in positive chastity, where the available psychic energy is all enlisted in the service of higher psychic activities. The chastity of the priest or nun has moral worth and meaning only if it is seen as a means towards enlisting the maximum of psychic energy in the service of the spiritual life. It is reprehensible whenever it is required as an independent and self-sufficient objective. The Church's teaching in this matter is in perfect harmony with the findings of depth psychology. If it happens that certain Church superiors demand a purely material chastity from the seminarian or priest or religious, without being too concerned over the purposes this chastity is to serve, this must be regarded as a simple — but very dangerous — misunderstanding of the Church's teaching.

No matter what motives lead him to observe chastity, the individual must realize that he can avoid the effects of this practice only by sublimating the energy he thus leaves unused. The techniques of this sublimation are quite variable, according to circumstances and individual cases. An intense spiritual

life, intellectual work, involvement in the creative arts, enthusiastic sports activity — all these are, in different degrees,
effective ways to put the libido and its psychic energy to good
use. Obviously, even the champion cyclist, the most fervent
mystic, the accomplished artist all can find it difficult to put
up with the demands of the sex instinct. It is all but impossible
to sublimate the total energy of the libido; a more or less
significant part of the energy will always remain vested in
the sex instinct. But in the case of persons such as these, the
unsublimated quantity is hardly ever a threat to the equilibrium
of the personality. Chastity, in such circumstances, can hardly
be a source of danger. Quite the contrary, it is a powerful
factor in promoting the fuller exercises of his higher psychic
activities.

For most adults, normal sexual activity is unquestionably
necessary for psychic equilibrium. It would be idle to hope that
just any person could be capable of sublimation to the degree
we have just described it. And on the other hand some degree
of chastity is absolutely indispensable for every person who
does not want to sink into utter dissipation.

Whatever might be the psychological and even physiological
disadvantages of chastity without intensive sublimation, we
definitely have to admit that the evils flowing from sexual
abandon are infinitely more serious. And, in the last analysis,
sexual abandon is the only adequate term to describe someone
who turns to sexual satisfaction every time he feels the impulse
and the occasion presents itself.

In my experience as a psychologist, I have encountered
neurotic patients whose conflicts were closely bound up with
the brutal repression of their sex instincts. But I have seen even
more examples of those whose neurosis, particularly in the case
of obsessional neurosis, was either caused, in the proper sense
of the term, or at least aggravated, by sexual abuse. Men and
women who would have been capable of realizing what we
generally call an "authentic existence," a life that is both indi-

vidually and socially of a higher order, have been condemned by their sexual excesses to a life of mediocrity or even moral degeneracy. The totality of their psychic energy was broken by the overactivity of their sexual impulses, and there was no psychic libido left to supply the life of the mind or the call to action.

## III. Sex and Love

The proponents of a certain type of biologism, long outmoded on the scientific plane, still like to exaggerate the similarities between animal and human sexuality. Would it be equally reasonable, in their eyes, to suppose that since the baby begins his career by emitting only inarticulate sounds, there is no radical distinction between human and animal speech?

It is not impossible that, even in the case of certain higher animals, the sex instinct is something more than simply biological in nature. This is certainly true in the case of man. The more a man succeeds in humanizing himself, the greater the role that his psychic powers will have to play in his sex life. Whereas the animal is immediately ordered towards procreation, sexual power in the human person, once he is civilized and cultured, tends less and less exclusively to be occupied with this social objective and turns more and more explicitly into a noble symbol and an expression of the interpersonal community of love. The energy that is released by sexuality in the human person is only partially biological, the rest remains psychic in nature. Thus, in order for sexuality to play the role it ought to play in promoting the development of equilibrium in the human person, it is necessary to satisfy both flesh and spirit as well. This more than any other single factor is a clear indication of the twofold nature of man — flesh and spirit.

The human sex act should never take place between a man and woman who are not in love with each other. This does not mean that it always needs to be accomplished by the great passion of love which is the hallmark of romanticism. For the purposes under discussion here, such love need be, basically, no more than the fruit of mutual respect or a feeling of tenderness and affection. What counts is the fact that two hearts, and two bodies, go out towards each other. Obviously, the closer this union of hearts, the closer also and the more dignified and human will be the physical embrace of love. Human beings "make love," whereas animals are said to copulate. Every time a man and woman complete the sex act without love, they are merely copulating, which is to say that they are becoming more like animals, losing something of their human dignity. In the eyes of simple or backward people, the mere accomplishment of the physical act might seem to be enough to satisfy the impulse of the sex instinct. But in the case of mere refined and sensitive men and women, the mere physical act always leaves something unsatisfied, and frequently painfully so.

Charles, a bachelor of 26, showed clear signs of anxiety: he did not sleep well and he had trouble keeping his mind on his work at the office. The doctor he consulted thought that the cause of his troubles lay in the fact that he had been a bachelor too long. Consequently, since the young man had no available girl friends, he advised him to visit a house of prostitution. Charles followed the advice. His tensions were considerably relieved, but only for a time and then they reappeared under a much more acute form. When he tried to repeat the advice again, the same remedy proved to be less and less effective, until finally it offered no relief at all.

During the course of a competent psychotherapy which he subsequently underwent, it turned out that the first doctor's diagnosis was correct enough, but the measures he prescribed were not at all proper. What Charles really needed was not just intercourse, but love. It was much more difficult to bear up under the physical tension resulting from the denial of sex than it was to face the prospect of emotional solitude. Obviously the girls he visited in the brothel had nothing to offer in the way of real affection for him, and thus Charles only felt his loneliness all the more each time he tried the remedy. He gradually slipped into a neurosis of acute depression.

Not all men experience the same dramatically unfortunate results from visiting a brothel. But neither does such an outlet ever really respond to all the specifically human elements of sexual relations. Many husbands who complain of frigidity in their wives are really to blame themselves. Initiated to sex by relations with a prostitute or at best in some other atmosphere that was totally lacking in real affection, they can only adopt a similar technique and attitude towards their new bride. They end up treating her as if she too were no more than a pander to their physical pleasure. This does not keep them from loving their wives, but their love has no real effect on their sexual behavior. And in the woman, much more explicitly than in the man, love is indissolubly bound up with the sex impulse: if love is missing, there will necessarily always be something really missing in the physical experience as well.

### IV. Marriage or "Free Love"?

Habit, routine, too great a sense of security — these are all difficult trials for married love. Sexual intercourse runs the risk of losing its spontaneity, and ceasing to be a free gift springing from untrammelled love: it tends to turn into the accomplishment of what has been unfortunately called "conjugal duty." In an attempt to escape these unwelcome consequences, many married people, particularly during the first quarter of this century, became proponents of so-called "free love." Free love, as they saw it, was to be an almost automatic solution to the difficulties inherent in the institution of marriage.

The proponents of this solution thought that in the absence of any formal bond and juridic contract, a man and woman could no longer rely on a dangerous sense of security but would always have to be on guard to keep the flame of their love from faltering. And if the understanding between them — carnal or moral — becomes something truly impossible, there is nothing to keep the partners from separating. This would eliminate the problems arising from unhappy marriages, in which the man or woman are chained together like galley slaves. Obviously there would be a problem of children, in case of such a separation. But this would be a problem only in a capitalist society: in a socialist regime the State would take over the job of bringing them up. It was only logical that the sympathies of such people naturally turned towards Communism . . . .

Psychology cannot help recognize the justness of some of the arguments advanced by the adversaries of marriage as an institution. It is beyond argument, for instance, that a sense of security can easily be a real danger to married love. But it would be most rash to conclude that only free love offers an effective remedy against this threat, and there is no psychological basis for the statement.

There is no room here to discuss all the various overtones that the relationship of human love can take in the distant future. Based solely on the observations of personal experience, a psychologist might well be forced to recognize the fact that only a very few people can manage to live in a relationship of free love without danger. These dangers are not all the fault of the Christian *superego*, so frequently abused and misunderstood by many modern writers. People who deliberately reject every moral system that is Christian in inspiration do not, for all that, manage to make a satisfactory life out of free love any more than true Christians would.

Russian communism, as everyone knows, was, originally, in perfect sympathy with the principles of free love; it seemed to offer an indispensable complement to the economic and social liberation of humanity. But a dozen years' experience were enough to convince the leaders of the Soviet Union that the remedy was, in this case, worse than the disease. The government of the U.S.S.R. was concerned primarily with all the evil consequences of free love in the collective social order. But there were a good many Soviet poets and novelists to describe the harm it did on the individual psychological plane.

There need be no surprise in the fact that the effects of free love are much more detrimental to women than they are to men. It might well be true that they run less risk of turning into unbearable nags than they would in the security of marriage. But, at the end of a certain number of such extramarital experiences, they almost always turn into a psychic wreck, which is hardly more desirable. The extraordinary number of women who committed suicide in the U.S.S.R. when free love was the accepted practice there, was one of the very first danger signs that the public officials noted. The psychologist could not help but see it as a sign of a terrible disorder. Love, to be authentic, necessarily implies the generous giving of self. In the face of repeated refusal to give and take this complete gift, it is impossible for a human person to retain anything of his faith in love as such, and, as a consequence, in himself. Suicide is a logical end result.

Julie was not a Soviet citizen: she lived in Paris. She was the daughter of free thinkers and no Christian or other religious influence had ever figured in her education. When, at the age of 15, she had her first love affair, her parents considered her behavior perfectly normal and were not at all upset. At the age of 17, she began living with a man who was considerably older than she. Six months later, she left him because she had discovered "real love" in the person of a man who was much younger, and much richer. But, two years later, this young man left her, to marry a rich heiress. After a painful crisis of loneliness and rejection that lasted for about a year, she formed another liaison, but this time she had no particular expectation or even any hope that it would last very long. As it actually worked out, Julie left her companion a few months later; he had suddenly become enamoured of a younger woman. Abandoned and humiliated, the poor woman tried to take her life. The doctor who saved her life afterwards sent her to see a psychologist. The psychologist had little to work on in her case: she no longer believed in anything and she had no love for anyone, not even herself.

Obviously, free love is not always going to produce such dire results in every case. Still, I could easily point out a number of examples of the destructive effects it has on even the so-called stronger sex. The uncertainty and anxiety necessarily involved in free love are no more likely to promote the development of human personality — masculine or feminine — than the lazy feeling of security.

Thus it would seem that it is not the abolition of marriage that we must look to as a remedy against the undeniable defects that are only too obvious in the majority of marital unions sanctioned by church and state, but rather an intrinsic re-evaluation of the marriage state.

## V. Prerequisites for a Happy Marriage

There is no secret anywhere that can guarantee the happiness of marriage. The fact that two people feel attracted to each other and decide to live together as man and wife depends at least to some extent on unconscious factors that are beyond the free control of the individual involved. As a result, many marriages that have given much promise at the outset turn out very badly, even though all the psychological factors seem to have been taken into account. It is with this note of reserve that the following "preliminaries" must be read and understood.

First of all, marriage should not begin at too early an age. Before entering into a serious existential communion with another person, a man needs to have acquired his full maturity in both the intellectual and emotional orders, the maximum of personal independence. Otherwise there is real danger that his further development will merely follow the lead set by his partner; he might become merely an image of her, or she of him, incapable of offering the stimulus and "otherness" that the partner also needs for further development. This danger is always greater in the case of a husband and wife who are lacking in real maturity. There is some chance that they will begin to develop in opposite directions.

Farm people and working class people generally attain their full psychological maturity towards the age of legal maturity. There is nothing here to counter-indicate marriage at about the age of twenty. But things are quite different in the case of those who have been to high school and college. Because of the very nature of their education and the time they spend acquiring it, they have only a very meager experience in the affairs of the world before the end of their formal education. Consequently, early marriages between students are generally not advantageous and as a general rule they are to be discouraged. Moreover, the kind of maturity required in a doctor, an engineer, or a professor, is something very different from the maturity expected in a farmer or workingman. The degree of maturity the working class man achieves at twenty is not generally possible for the professional person before the age of thirty. This, consequently, might be considered the best age for marriage in their case.

Things are somewhat different in the case of women who have had an opportunity to go to college. Naive and innocent "little brides" are no longer any match for the complex demands of modern marriage. This is not to deny the equally certain fact that many young ladies do not really "become themselves" until they find a man to love them. This in turn would seem to justify a certain leeway in the age difference of the two partners.

It is just as obvious that late marriages have their dis-advantages too. But these disadvantages, at least on the objective plane, seem to be considerably less serious. Nor must any of the preceding be construed as an attempt to advise people to wait until they reach forty before they marry.

* * *

Ideally speaking, there should only be marriages of love. This is not the place to reopen the age-old controversy about "marriages of reason" and "marriages of love." Possibly, there was a time when marriages of reason did correspond to the conditions of human life as it actually existed. But it is obviously true that such a marriage no longer answers the emotional needs of men and women of our own day and civilization. The cause for this is probably the extraordinary development of individual awareness in this century, together with a strong regression of community awareness. It is becoming more and more difficult to find a case in which a couple can marry, without some serious damage, solely in the interests of family or name. Marriage for money is still a factor in their marriage. Marriage can really succeed only if it is based on mutual love.

The most important element in this whole consideration is that young people (and their parents and counsellors) must get used to making the proper distinctions between real love and its ephemeral counterpart, generally known under the name of infatuation or "being thunderstruck." Real love always implies a deep communion, both of flesh and spirit, between two persons: and this in turn requires the full emotional maturity of the two persons. Without such maturity, men and women who are too young, as well as adults who are not really mature, will almost always mistake this superficial infatuation for a true love. In this pseudo-love, the only mutual attractions are physical: by its very nature it cannot last, unless a real communion of spirit also develops to give it the needed strength.

But it is just as important to be on guard against an excessive idealization of love. In certain groups of young Christians especially, there is a tendency to put so much stress on the spiritual side of love that a great many young brides find themselves frankly embarrassed by the carnal aspects of marriage. They believe that they loved the man they married because they shared the same religious ideal, because they were "fellow Christians" together, because they liked the same poets and the same musicians. But once they are married they frequently find no physical attraction for their husband; sometimes it is even a sense of repugnance that they feel. Young people must not be kept misinformed about the importance of this physical attraction.

Michelle, after ten years of marriage, was abandoned by her husband who claimed that she did not love him enough. She was completely dumbfounded by his reasons: she knew that she had married solely out of love, even against her parents' advice and her own best material interests. The psychologist with whom she discussed her misfortune very quickly discovered the nature of the mistake she had made. The love she had felt for the man who was to become her husband was made up of a mixture of pity and motherly tenderness and affection for a young man who had no mother and was being mistreated by his stepmother. This feeling she had managed to sublimate to a very high degree, by an attitude, often mistakenly called Christian, of self-sacrifice in the interests of "one she loved." She had never had any interest in, or paid any attention to, the young man's body; at least she never felt any attraction for him in this area.

Obviously things could have worked out in such a way that married life itself would have given rise to this physical attraction between Michelle and her husband. Actually, there are a good number of young ladies who, before marriage, had never experienced any more physical attraction than did Michelle; but they develop fully, in and through marriage. Such, unfortunately, was not true in the case of Michelle and she was left abandoned and overcome with shock at the ruins of her once great love.

Equally as pernicious is the idea that certain young brides have of marriage, conceived of exclusively as a legitimate and virtuous means to have children. They naturally tend to choose as their husband the man whom they want to be the father of their children, without being too much concerned with him as a husband and lover. Only very infrequently, after the birth of the first child, will such a bride have any absorbing interest in marriage; she will more or less feel that her husband has accomplised his mission in marriage and now has but one single "right," namely to provide food and shelter for his wife and the children.

Obviously, the husband cannot find happiness in such an atmosphere. But it also happens frequently enough that a woman who has married "a father for her children" will one day manage to discover the man for whom her heart and body long. Then she is in danger of sacrificing everything to her new found passion — home, children, and ideals — and destroying what she would have, up to that moment, considered as the very essence of her vocation in life.

## VI. Wedding Night

Very many of the young brides who need a psychologist's help are those whose neurosis is closely bound up with their first sexual experience, that is, in most cases, on their wedding night. Their fundamental trauma obviously dates much farther back in their experience, either in adolescence or childhood. But it is very probable that if the experience of their wedding night had not been so disastrous, the traumas would never have so seriously disturbed their psyche, and, as a consequence, the happiness of their married life.

Most people might think it hardly possible that, in our day and age, some young brides can arrive at the age for marriage with an almost complete ignorance of the nature of sexual relations. But there are still very many young brides of whom this is true, even among those who have been to college. In some cases this is the result of total lack of information on the part of educators. Still a careful analysis of the situation reveals the fact that more and more frequently, particularly among educated and cultured women, it is the activity of the superego that is responsible, a superego which for centuries has been trained to look down on sex. This factor then makes it impossible for them to make a proper application of their theoretical knowledge to their own emotional life and circumstances. I have known some young brides who were doctors, perfectly acquainted with the physiology of sex and capable of discussing sex with an almost excessive freedom, and yet at the moment of their marriage, they turned out to be as ignorant and backward as the most ignorant country girl, or even more so. Their superego would not allow them to apply what they had learned in their books and in their clinics, to their own sex life.

There is some grounds to hope that this state of affairs will change for a future generation of brides who are the young girls of today. In some well-informed circles, mothers are becoming more and more conscious of the unwholesome character of this form of "innocence" and determined not to allow their daughters to continue in an ignorance that has been the cause of so much suffering in their own lives. Obviously, the fight against the superego will be a more difficult one. But there are many priests and many parents today who are in tune with the dangers presented by making sex something to feel guilty about. They are taking a stand against the problem, and there is every hope that, little by little, the superego will have to yield some ground.

Whether we are speaking of the brides of today or those who will be the brides of tomorrow (and we like to suppose that these last will have received a much better education on matters of emotion and sex), the man who initiates them to sex will always play a very big role in keeping the wedding night free of all traumatic effects.

It is most urgent for men to be convinced, once and for all, that, in the woman, sex is something fundamentally different than in the man. It makes little difference, for the purposes of this book, whether this radical difference is due to "nature" or the education that family and society insist on giving to young ladies. What must be recognized is the fact that most women are incapable of experiencing any pleasure and joy in *physical* love excepting through *psychic* love. At a time that is as important for their emotional life as their wedding night, it is not enough to *know*, rationally, that the man to whom they have given themselves really loves them: they have to *feel* this love, intensely. As a result, any violent or impatient behavior on his part is likely to appear as a lack of tenderness or even a lack of love, and the consequences can be very serious for the whole of their married life. Moreover, in order to create an emotionally propitious "climate," words are just as important as actions, for most women, and the words always have to set the stage for the actions.

Every doctor and psychologist knows the evil effects that inexperience on the husband's part will almost always have on married happiness. This is particularly true when both husband and wife are virgins on their wedding night. Some people condemn marriage of this kind out of hand, considering that it is absolutely indispensable for the future husband to have acquired sufficient experience in love and lovemaking. But such an opinion is obviously at variance with the moral precepts of many religions, particularly Catholic morality.

Keeping to his own field, the psychologist can only admit that a woman who marries a mature man, one who knows life and has a certain knowledge and experience of the woman's psychology, stands a much better chance of having a happy wedding night. But it would be a serious mistake to believe that such knowledge and experience has to do only with sex; a young man of 20 needs much more than a few sexual experiences to make his young bride happy on their wedding night. What is needed is really a general human experience and sex experience is only one of the integral elements.

On many occasions we have noted how the remedies recommended by certain "hygienists," that is, the previous sexual initiation of the husband, can have consequences every bit as disastrous as the evil they claim to combat. Such an initiation, obviously, will take place most of the time in the arms of a prostitute, quite divorced from any "climate of emotion or love." Such an experience could only warp the young man's ideas about love and women.

Whatever might be the disadvantages of marriage between virgins, they seem far less serious than those which could result from a poor "initiation." In the first case, there is every chance that, with the help of their mutual love, a bride and groom who are more or less normal will gradually discover a mutually satisfactory technique for themselves. But in the second hypothesis, there is some fear that the husband, particularly when he is young and lacking in psychological penetration, will experience only an extreme disillusionment, because his wife is "not as good" as the prostitute. As for the bride, she is almost always hurt, and to the very depths of her deepest sensitivities, by the overly brutal behavior of such a husband. Such a misunderstanding, at the beginning of the marriage, will rarely, if ever, work itself out without help: most of the time, it will poison the sex relations (and thus, to a great degree, the mutual love) of the young couple for a long time to come, if not permanently.

In any hypothesis, it is very important for the young people to know that successful love-making is not something to be learned on a single wedding night. In a more general way, we might point out that the wedding night is not a particularly good occasion for sexual initiation. The fatigue after the wedding ceremony and reception almost always increases the natural anxiety at approaching an act whose importance is already greatly exaggerated by the imagination. Thus it is no wonder that the highly praised wedding night is frequently a real failure.

Many doctors and psychologists, aware of the psychological complications of the wedding night, that is, the first sexual relations at a fixed date and hour, advise the "consummation" of the marriage before its "consecration." In some frequently Christian circles, where there can be no question of pre-martial sexual experiences, even with an engaged couple, it has become a practice not to consummate the marriage until several days after the ceremony. Either of these two expedients can equally help the first physical union between the husband and wife to take place spontaneously and thus alleviate much of the anxiety that the young bride normally experiences at the approach of an event which apears to be so mysterious to her.


## VII. Faithfulness in Love

There is an almost universal conviction that the sex instinct, at least in the male, is by its nature, polygamous. This is partially true, but always with the proviso that human sexuality is not solely a matter of the sex instinct, but is equally bound up with human love, and that the laws of the one are not necessarily valid for the other. Whether it be a man or woman under discussion, love does not admit of being shared. Love, when it is true love, is capable of serving as perfect counterbalance to the fundamental anarchy of the sex instinct.

Still, experience teaches us that, after a certain number of years of married life, even the man who is most sincerely in love with his wife will notice that his wife has less sexual appeal for him than many other women who might well be much less charming, objectively speaking, and for whom he feels no particular love or affection. It seems that the psychological explanation of this often very painful phenomenon is to be found in the fundamentally aggressive nature of sex in the male. Despite civilization and culture, on this plane, man has remained basically the "primitive savage" who feels the urge and the desire to subdue his woman by physical strength. The woman's typical shyness and coquetry always make this attitude more or less necessary, even if fashions have changed somewhat.

In the first days of his married life, a man might experience genuine content at not having to wage a constant struggle in order to have some satisfaction for sexual urgency. But little by little, for lack of fuel to his aggressive instincts, he begins to find conjugal sex rather insipid and realizes that he is more and more attracted by other women, women who are still to be "conquered." In the case of many men, particularly those who have strong moral and religious convictions or who have a really deep love for their wives, this impulse never reaches adultery. They are content to flirt with these other women or use the brilliance of their wit and the paradoxical sparkle of their conversation as a seductive spell for others. The intellectual will be satisfied with making fervent disciples. But even virtuous men will sometimes go beyond the stage of play-acting and commit adultery, and frequently destroy their homes.

From the point of view of mental health, these "centrifugal" tendencies of the sex instinct unquestionably involve some very real dangers. Many men have become prematurely impotent in their married sex relations. This impotence almost always gives rise to neurosis, leads to a loss of interest in the man's work, and presents an obstacle to all his undertakings: it is the direct cause of neurasthenia and depression.

Whether under the pressure of unconscious social inhibitions or "by nature," the woman seems more spontaneously monogamous. Still, it happens often enough that married life, in the long run, is no more satisfying for her than for the man. If she has been roused to sexual pleasure from the very first days of her marriage, it is very rare for her to lose her aptitude to experience orgasm in her husband's embrace, even if relations between the two have become devoid of all true affection. Unfortunately, and generally through the husband's fault, very many women never do experience this orgasm. What they are looking for more than anything else in sexual relations is tenderness and affection, their pleasure being much more sentimental than sexual. What is more, even those who have experienced orgasm are at least as hungry for sentiment and open affection as the others. This fact is, in its root, intimately bound up with the woman's predominantly passive sexuality. Just as the male has a need to conquer and overcome, the woman wants to be conquered and possessed. In only one respect do their roles seem to be really inverse: whereas the man needs to be admired by the woman he loves, the woman needs to be able to admire the object of her love.

In many families, the woman very quickly receives the impression that she is no longer really conquered or possessed, but simply had as an object, and this in virtue of the so-called marital rights which have nothing very much in common with real love. On the other hand, all too often her admiration for her husband cannot stand up against the trials of everyday living: her husband looked like a real man and gentleman before and now he shows more and more signs of mediocrity.

The proportion of women married over ten years who are

emotionally unsatisfied or even unhappy is really surprising. Some women look for, and perhaps even find, some outside satisfaction, if not in a genuine extra marital love, at least by flirting, not at all unlike the behavior of the "virtuous" husband described above.

Others however, and probably the majority, direct their whole need to love and be loved upon their children. They turn into real "mother hens" or, to put it into the terminology of psychoanalysis, they become *overweening* or *devouring* mothers. Such a mother's love — which often looks like something heroic but is really almost always something egotistical — presents a serious obstacle to the maturity of the children. Such a love is really neurotic in essence, just as the exaggerated need to flirt is also generally neurotic, and the half-desires that many women have to commit adultery.

A third category is made up of those who can discover the satisfaction they crave neither in their need for tenderness and affection nor in flirting or exaggerated mother's love. Their only refuge is in neurosis, a neurosis whose symptoms are obviously much more serious.

What is to be done to remedy such a lamentable and often catastrophic situation? It is at this point that mental hygiene has to intervene.

### VIII. *Preserving Love*

To begin with, every effort must be made to keep sex from cheapening by the very routine of married life. Intimacy is never synonymous with promiscuity; quite the contrary, promiscuity is very harmful to real marital intimacy. The psychologist can only regret that present-day living conditions make it impossible for most married couples to have separate bedrooms. Obviously it would be ridiculous to see this as a panacea for all the disadvantages which spring from the easy accessibility of physical love in the married state. But on the concrete plane of everyday life, we must be satisfied with what we can have, and it would be worth while to have at least some small degree of help in securing such an important goal.

The next objective would be to set up a far-reaching and persevering education effort to make the notions of conjugal duty and conjugal right completely disappear from the spoken vocabulary and from the unconscious minds of married couples. These juridic concepts can only work serious harm when they are applied to an area which is concerned solely with love. By being convinced to the very depths of his understanding and feeling that conjugal intimacy has nothing to do with either rights or duties, a man might perhaps feel that he is bound to conquer and possess his wife all over again, even after long years of marriage. He would have to make a real effort to deserve her admiration, every day, all over again.

John and Annette had been married for eight years when I first made their acquaintance at a dinner party in a friend's home. John was a brilliant conversationalist, very outgoing and very much a man of the world. Annette was outstanding for her elegance, and her remarkable capacity to take an interest in the conversation even when her table companion was talking about something that she knew absolutely nothing about. Everyone considered them a perfectly matched couple. The two women on either side of John, seemed to be saying to themselves: "If only I had a husband like that!," while Annette's table companions could not help being jealous of, or happy for, the lucky husband of "such a wonderful woman."

A few weeks after this dinner party, I learned that John and Annette were getting along very poorly together. From consultation I learned that at home he was moody and taciturn, and that for many years he had not bothered to show his wife any tenderness or even the most elementary politeness. In his sex relations with her his attitude was that of a man who is confident of his rights and her duties: his only object was to satisfy his own desires. As for Annette, at home she was nothing at all like the living woman I had met at the dinner party. She was slow to get up in the morning and made a project out of getting desssed: she would come down to breakfast without combing her hair, without any make-up, in her robe and slippers. Is it any wonder that this young couple no longer felt any sexual attraction for each other? Little by little, they had come to despise each other.

Another serious obstacle to love in married life consists, as we have already alluded, in the fact that the satisfaction of the sexual desire in marriage is too easy. Sex pleasure, as everyone knows, is proportional to the intensity of the sexual tension that has preceded it. Too many married people do not make the necessary effort to bring this tension to an intense enough level. The result is actual frigidity in the case of women who are not at all frigid physically, and, in the husband, the impression that he can enjoy only mediocre pleasure with his wife. The search for a more intense form of sex pleasure is the basis of most conjugal infidelity.

Psychology, from its point of view, can only praise the demands of medieval morality that forbade married couples to have sexual relations during the season of Advent or Lent, during the Ember Days, and on certain other liturgical feast days throughout the year. Not that we think sexual indulgence goes counter to the greater purity of life that religion demands of its faithful under certain circumstances. But it is important for the love between husband and wife to retain a character of freshness and free giving, and it must never degencrate into mere routine. Now, experience has shown that temporary continence greatly promotes this state of affairs. The methods to be practiced in this respect will obviously vary according to persons and circumstances.

Thus, in certain circles of young Christian couples there is a growing practice of making separate annual retreats. Other couples experience a strong renewal of their mutual sexual attraction every month, after the strict observance of continence demanded by the practice of the rhythm system.

## IX. Love and Children

It is not within the framework of this book to discuss the sociological or moral aspects of married fecundity or sterility. The only thing that interests us here is their psychological aspect, that is, the repercussion they have on the happiness and normal development of the individuals.

Normally, children are an essential element in the success of any married love. With the exception of couples who are so fundamentally self-centered (and there are very few of these) that they can think only of their own personal pleasure, young married people are generally somewhat concerned if, at the end of a few months of married life, a baby is not yet on the way. Even couples who have good reasons for not desiring any children — at least for the time being, or even indefinitely — always need to know that they are still capable of having them. The result is a situation that is sometimes practically hopeless.

The arrival of the first child is thus welcomed with joy in almost all families, even where difficult living conditions might have led the couple to prefer a long period of waiting. Unconsciously, husband and wife seem to see a sort of consecration or confirmation of their own love in the birth of the child. What is more, the philosophers have long seen creativity as the fundamental characteristic of all true love. Whenever the mutual love of husband and wife corresponds to the criteria we have described above, the birth of a child will reinforce the bond that joins them. It is not at all rare, either, for the advent of the first child to repair what was initially imperfect and lacking in their love.

Problems and difficulties generally begin to appear with the second or third pregnancy. In the light of experience, it is not good, for the husband and wife, for pregnancies to follow each other too closely. The material demands which result from having a child are often too heavy to be anything other than a real burden upon the harmony of the household. The wife, even the most amorous, will easily let herself be monopolized by her obligations as a mother and thus run the risk of no longer being so attentive to the legitimate and normal physical demands of her husband.

Even a couple with the most ardent desire for a large family will do well to space their children. However, all too frequently the desire for a large family has secret roots deep in the unconscious sense of guilt in the face of everything relating to sex. The children are then less desired for their own sakes than as a means to free the parents from this anxiety — an expedient which seldom works. It would be much better, both for husband and wife themselves and for the children, if the sexual expression of their married life could become a positive element in promoting their mutual love.

In the present-day conditions of existence and with the present level of development of the individual conscience, the psychologist must unhesitatingly stand up for the principle of voluntary parenthood. In theory, it is possible to look back with fond recollections on days gone by when people considered life in general and married life in particular with that passive spirit of submission to fatality which has been mistakenly christened "Providence." In those days, people were resigned easily enough to facing the "law of nature" in respect to birth and babies. The same is no longer true for men of today, who have been educated in the cult of individual liberty. Rightly or wrongly, they no longer consider anything good or beautiful unless it is the product of their own free choice. Now psychology has nothing to say about the eternal essences of things: it is the individual man, as he exists here and now, who is the only proper object of psychological research and theorizing.

It is not our purpose here to recommend any one particular method of controlling the number and spacing of births in marriage. From our point of view, the only methods that deserve to be condemned out of hand are those which involve an emotional shock, a risk of psychic trauma. Moreover, we can only rejoice at the fact that even an institution as firmly attached to traditional morality as the Catholic Church, seems, by her advocation of the rhythm system, to support the principle of voluntary and responsible parenthood. This is nothing more, for the present, than a preliminary step; but it should be enough to divest sex of its magical and mysterious character and bring people to look upon it no longer solely, or even primarily, as a natural instinct tending towards the procreation of the human species.

# 6 the age of retirement

It might seem to be a contradiction of certain theoretical views, but every practicing psychologist knows from experience that the emotional shock which precipitates a neurosis can occur even in old age — an age in which the individual might expect to find himself sheltered from any new disturbances, when the only maladies that threaten his existence are the infirmities of age.

## I. Involutional Neurosis

Helen had had an unhappy childhood and adolescence; she had suffered many traumas which might have easily disposed her to neurosis. Then she managed to hit upon a profession which fitted her perfectly and made the conditions of her existence very favorable. As a result, throughout her adult life, she never showed any symptoms that were specifically neurotic enough to demand professional treatment. She did seem a little bit strange to some of her friends at times. Her moodiness, her natural inclination to be discouraged, her awkward way of expressing herself and her frequent sharp sarcasm went far beyond what might be considered normal conduct in this area. But all this did not keep her from successfully meeting the demands of her professional and family life.

Like so many other women, she began to withdraw from people at about the age of 55 and this proved to be the comptele ruin of her personality. The victim of obsessions and hallucinations, she had to be treated several times by electric shock.

Long before the discoveries of psychoanalysis, people were well aware of the fact that women, between the ages of 40 and 50, go through a difficult period, called the crisis of menopause. This crisis has much in common with the earlier crisis of puberty. In the case of women who are predisposed to neurosis (even if, as in the case of Helen, they have long resisted the latent threats) the crisis of menopause can easily take on a much more serious character: this is the involutional neurosis which we shall have to discuss at length.

In normal women, the crisis of menopause, on the psychic plane, does not involve any more than the simple repercussion normal to all physiological transformations; there is no particular danger here. After a more or less lengthy period of troubles, these women recover their normal equilibrium. It would be absurd to treat every woman who passes through menopause as a neurotic. But involutional neurosis, on the other hand, does present a serious threat for those women in whom neurosis has been latent since childhood. The defense mechanisms which the ego had succeeded in setting up against neurosis are all swept away by the crisis of menopause: such women often become the prey of psychic disease.

Frequently, involutional neurosis begins its onslaught several years before the menopause as such; we then speak of a pre-menopause neurosis. The symptoms of involutional neurosis are not specific. Depending on the circumstances, it can assume the whole gamut of neuroses known to psychologists and psychiatrists. But it almost always takes on these symptoms in an appreciably more serious and acute manner than they would appear in an earlier stage of life. The cure of such a patient is always difficult, and sometimes even impossible. But since the psychologist can foretell, with something very much like certitude, that a given woman is running the risk of involutional neurosis, preventive care seems most desirable and that before the age of 35, whenever possible.

## II. Psychic Dangers to the Retired

Towards the age of 50, many men experience discomfort and troubles that are quite similar to those of the woman's menopause: headache, dizzy spells, moodiness, discouragement, etc. These problems hardly ever take on a really neurotic form, probably the organic modifications in the aging male are not at all so revolutionary as in the woman.

In the social life of men, the one great event that takes place at this time of life, on the psychic plane, is retirement from professional activity. This experience frequently results in psychic problems such as depression, loss of interest in living, excessive irritability, etc. Suicides, apparently without reason, are relatively frequent among retired people. Since their profession makes up a considerably lesser element of their life, women who retire do not generally face a similar danger, even if they have worked all their life and are genuinely absorbed in their work.

For some twenty years now, as a result of legislation and medical progress, the situation has become appreciably worse. We are obviously not contesting the excellence and advantage of this legislation and progress. But what is important is for men to be able to adapt their way of living to the new conditions they have to face.

In many professions, the age of retirement is legally set at 55. Two or three generations ago, most men felt "old" at that age. But today, thanks to the progress of medicine, improved nutrition, and better working conditions, no man who is normally healthy can consider himself, or deserve to be considered, an old man at the age of 55. He is enjoying his full maturity, his creative faculties have attained their optimum development. Isn't it rather odd that we consider it normal for the heads of some of the greatest states to be governed by men of 70 or 80, while the slightest effort with a pencil eraser is beyond the strength of a man of 55?

What can the retired man do with all the leisure time he now has at his disposal? It is not very often that he can find a new line of work, even part-time; only younger men can count on being hired. Experience shows that almost all men, after they no longer have anything specific to do, feel that they are useless, get bored, and very quickly decline into a senile neurosis whose most obvious symptoms are sadness, depression, peevishness, and a negatively critical attitude towards other people and the problems of existence. Everyone has known men over 60 who were still completely absorbed in some work, and as a result much "younger" than retired men of the same age. Physical senescence is much more frequently the consequence of psychic senescence than its cause.

What can be done to alleviate this unfortunate state of affairs? Is the psychologist to take a stand against social progress and campaign for a movement to put off the age of retirement?

Perhaps it would be desirable, in the case of the many professions or small businesses which make only relatively small demands on a man's strength, for the age of retirement to be provisionally at least, put off for about five more years. The intellectual level and the whole way of life of businessmen, research chemists, policemen, office personnel, etc., are generally such that retirement is particularly catastrophic for them.

The initiative in such a movement would have to come from the businessmen themselves; otherwise the proposal would look like social regression. The over-all duration of professional activity, however, must not be prolonged, at any price. As we have described above, in an effort to overcome the disadvantages of excessive specialization, specialized studies and also the age at which a profession is officially taken up ought to be extended to a much later age than is customary today, in order to make room for a more prolonged general education.

We must have no illusions about such a measure. It would be only a very partial remedy for the dangers inherent in the very situation of retirement. Whether retirement lasts a long or short time is obviously important: but it is much more important to teach men how to derive the fullest possible profit from it. These are only conditions that can keep people from being disturbed at the prospect of being forced to enter retirement.

It might well seem a paradox that we should speak of being disturbed at the prospect of retirement. Particularly when we consider how many young people let themselves be guided in the choice of a career towards government service, for example, especially because of the fine prospects of early retirement it offers.

The psychologist cannot be satisfied with such superficial motives. He will need only a bit of probing in the unconscious to discover that what makes such lines of work particularly attractive to so many young people is primarily the hope (partially based on the certainty of early retirement) of escaping the insecurity of the working man's condition. In the days when only such lines of work offered the prospect of retirement, this fact alone put them on a higher social plane than their neighbors. Now that working men and factory employees have the same privileges, retirement has become a merely economic factor.

Working for dozens of years at the same monotonous job, most men will begin to speak of their approaching retirement as if it were a promised land, a very happy experience. Some of them are living only to reach that goal. The psychologist realizes, of course, that this apparent satisfaction, unconsciously, tends to reassure the person who is doing the talking. With only rare exceptions, most men are somewhat afraid of the time when they will be free of their work.

And what is more, in the light of experience, such a fear is not ungrounded. How many professors, businessmen, and public figures are optimistic and cheerful when they are active and then very quickly become morose and dissatisfied as soon as they start their retirement. Without any taste for life, sunk in melancholy, they soon grow old, beset by every kind of psychic and physiological problem. Some of them die after just a few months, although there was nothing about their physical health that would make such an early death likely or foreseeable. In fact, it might well seem that the more active and intense a man's working life has been, the more dangerous are the effects of retirement.

### III. Excessive Interest in a Profession

There is no denying the fact that the role of professional activity is far too important in the life of many of our contemporaries. Government officials who can find relaxation in poetry, industrial figures who can enjoy painting on Sundays, doctors who have a passion for their collections of flowers or insects, workingmen who cultivate their own little garden — such men are becoming far too rare. But the man who is interested only in his job, who knows nothing but his job, is fatally uprooted and confused when he has to leave his professional activity. And just as a person who does nothing is already virtually dead (it is, after all, very true that life and activity go hand in hand), very frequently retirement comes only a few months before death.

Miss N. was a remarkable history teacher. She was not content with merely teaching her subject, but she was also interested in each of her pupils. She would invite them to visit her, she initiated them to the joys of intellectual work, she opened up all sorts of new horizons for them. But since she lived only for her work, the prospect of retirement looked like a terrible threat, even many years before it arrived. Every time she thought of it, a terrible anxiety came over her, enough to make her breathing difficult and disturb her normal heartbeat.

When the dreaded event finally arrived, it was a catastrophe. She no longer knew what to do: she stayed home all day long alone. No longer outgoing and charming, she was always melancholy: she let the housework go, she spent the whole day dressed only in an old bathrobe and slippers. After just six months of this new kind of living, Miss N. died from a bad case of flu. Those who knew her best all thought, and rightly so, that she had simply let herself die because life had no more meaning for her.

Not too many years ago, when the average working day was twelve hours, it was all but inevitable for a man's business world to take over the major portion of his existence and interests. But this can no longer be the case today, with only eight hours or less a day and five days a week. In fact, the time is in sight when, thanks to the modern advances of automation, a man might well plan on working only five or six hours a day and four days a week. It even seems not improbable that the main concern of professional organizations, in the not too distant future, might well be, not to promote higher salaries and better working conditions for their members, but rather to teach them the proper way to use their leisure time. A solution to this new "social problem No. 1" will also resolve the agonizing problems of retirement. To tell the truth, these last problems will all disappear when professional activity begins to take its place as only one of the many and varied activities in a person's life. Then, when professional interests inevitably have to be replaced by something else, there will be much to choose from.

In one sense, the problems discussed here are much more

acute in the higher social echelons than in the case of manual laborers. Technical progress already permits the manual laborer to escape from much of what is drudgery in his work; the only problem left is to utilize his extra-professional leisure. On the other hand, businessmen, investors, researchers, successful doctors, etc., have less and less time for a private life of their own. Professional demands monopolize their time to the point where they are much less capable of making an intelligent use of their leisure when the circumstances allow. We see them sitting bored in night clubs, in casinos, and at resorts, unless they are satisfied to race along the roads in their new sports car. From these ranks of "elite" come most of the neurotics and suicides of retirement.

The excessive specialization that modern technology demands makes it difficult for many men who have responsible positions to develop any other centers of interest. What secondary or leisure activity, for instance, could an electronics engineer turn to during retirement? It would be utopian to look for an answer to this problem on the plane of professional activity itself. Technological progress makes such specialization more and more indispensable and more and more widespread. Only a broad and profound general education, acquired before the time of specialization, can possibly equip a man for the struggle he will inevitably have to wage against these dangers.

## IV. Hobbies

The answer to many of the problems of retirement, such as described above, depends on official legislation. It would be rather pointless to expect lawmakers to put off both the age at which professional activity is taken up and the dates of retirement. The university people do not seem to be particularly convinced, for the moment, that it is important to have a more extended general education before specialization begins. Meantime, the psychologist must be satisfied with remedies that are obviously not perfect, remedies whose application depends on the individual himself, on the family, or on the initiative of the small community or club.

Every person who is aware of the importance and urgency of protecting his psychic equilibrium, owes it to himself to be involved in something besides his profession. The more absorbing and interesting his profession, the more indispensable his need for some outside interest, some hobby or leisure occupation. We must come to look on retirement and the end of professional activity and interests, not as the end of our life, but rather as a long-awaited opportunity to devote ourselves, finally, to all the different occupations and studies which, for lack of time, we have been able to pursue only imperfectly before.

Mr. G. had been the director of an important business for 70 years. Despite his many professional duties, he was always very concerned with establishing good understanding and friendly relationship among his personnel. When he handed over the direction of the business to his son, Mr. G. was extremely happy at the opportunity to devote himself entirely to the many movements which work for the betterment of international relations. Obviously he did not feel that he had been put aside or that he had become useless by leaving his position at the factory. Quite the contrary, he felt that his professional activity had been an excellent training for the new activities which he soon came to see as the realization of all his higher aspirations.

Mr. A., a retired philosophy professor, a dozen years after his retirement, is even more occupied now than during his teaching career. He took up apiculture. He developed an avid interest in bees, and combined his interest with original scientific research into the life and habits of bees. This was the realization of one of his lifelong ambitions.

Neither Mr. G. or Mr. A. were victims of the dangerous "retirement complex." Fortunately, a rather large number of men and women have managed to find themselves in situations that are more or less similar. In an effort to check the evil results of the specialization that professional activity inevitably involves there needs to be a much more widespread interest in hobbies and the prudent use of leisure time. There is some indication that the young people of today are not too well aware of the usefulness of this advice: failure to acquire outside interests can only expose them to serious disappointments when they, in their turn, have reached the age of retirement.

### V. Old Maids

"Old maids" make up a particularly impressive percentage of involutional neurotics. Whereas mothers and grandmothers can always turn to their families after the time of menopause, and count on a great degree of involvement in the life and activities of children and grandchildren, old maids are much more inclined to see this time of life as a full halt to their activity: they thus offer very litle resistance to the inroads of neurosis.

Fortunately, the number of "old maids," in the traditional sense of the term, is gradually and noticeably diminishing. Young ladies are much less preoccupied with waiting for a husband. They study the same courses as boys do and consider it only normal to look for some professional activity which is in keeping with their taste and capacities. As a result, those who do not marry (excluding those who take up religious life,) never turn into those poor creatures that we used to find in almost every family, clinging to a married brother or sister, the object of so many clever stories and remarks that are more witty than charitable.

Whatever the difficulties and problems that the unmarried

woman has to face today, and no matter how unbearable her loneliness might seem to most people, she is generally capable of finding at least as much self-realization in her professional work as does the ordinary businessman — particularly when her profession involves some dedication to the service of the individual or common good. What is more, her wise use of leisure time makes it possible for her to find the necessary sublimation she needs to escape the perils of involutional neurosis.

Thus we might conclude, that, in our modern age, the problems of retirement are not appreciably different for women than they are for their male colleagues. This is true except for the fact that since they are more subject than men to the bio-physiological influences of this stage of life, they have a proportionally greater need to forearm themselves, as much as possible, against the dangerous feelings of emptiness and uselessness that go along with retirement.

# 7 mental hygiene and spiritual life

*I. Religion, the Opiate of the Sick Soul?*

There are very many unbelievers, and also very many believers, of all religious denominations, who more or less explicitly look upon religion, with its dogmas and rites, as a form of medicine for sick souls. It is not at all uncommon to hear an unhappy or troubled person say something like: "If only I had the faith, I would not have to undergo these torments .... I am suffering all this pain because I do not have the faith .... If I could believe in God, I would no longer be afraid to die, I would not have this terrible anxiety, I would not be so worked up about it." Many people do not realize that there can be neurotics even among those who believe. And many religious ministers like to make the statement that, "If you believe in God you will be delivered from all your anxieties, and you will have peace of soul."

Moreover, there are very many psychotherapists who have a tendency to look upon religious faith primarily, if not solely, as a more or less helpful adjunct to their own techniques. I know doctors, who while they are perfect agnostics themselves, "collaborate," as they put it, on a permanent basis, with priests and ministers, referring "for more complete treatment" those of their patients whom Freudian analysis had not helped to find the peace of mind they need.

The educated believer of our day, the man who really lives

his faith, obviously cannot allow religion to be turned into a mere anesthetic against the threat of psychic torment. This would be a justification of all the violent criticism on the part of men like Nietzsche. Religion is essentially a step upward from existence on a purely natural level to a supra-temporal plane, an elevation to a supra-historical and thus necessarily supra-psychological level.

Moreover, simple intellectual honesty would oblige us to admit that neurotics are not all bad people, that really devout people can also be neurotics. In some cases, in fact, it would seem that it is precisely their religious life that is the cause of their neurosis. It is true, of course, that in most such cases, we are speaking not of an authentically theological faith, but rather of bigotry, fetishism, or superstition masquerading as religion.

## II. Faith and Neurosis

Religion is thus not essentially an antidote nor an antiseptic against neurosis. There is no real foundation in the fear of certain of the faithful, who appear to have been too much influenced by the popular concepts of Freud's teaching, that psychotherapy, particularly under the form of psychoanalysis, is going to destroy their faith. In experiencing and expressing such a fear, such believers are actually, without knowing it, giving substance to the thesis of those thinkers who deny any fundamental distinction between religion on the one hand and superstition or fetishism on the other.

I must admit that I have known persons who claim they have lost their faith as a result of successful psychoanalysis. But it always turns out that when I dig into their background a bit, I discover that they have never had real faith, that what they called their faith was really only an integral part of their neurosis and thus obviously could only be expected to disappear with the neurosis itself.

André, 24, was a seminarian. Anxious and scrupulous, he could no longer either work or pray, nor even sleep. With the permission of his superiors, he went to an excellent psychoanalyst for help. The analysis was long and difficult. Finally, when the psychotherapy had succeeded in restoring André's psychic equilibrium, the young man no longer had the least desire to be a priest. He left the seminary and abandoned all his religious practices.

Was it psychoanalysis that destroyed André's faith? The head of the seminary and André's parents liked to think so, without realizing that by so thinking they were crediting psychoanalysis with a much exaggerated power over a reality which they otherwise considered to be trans-phenomenal and thus beyond the reach of psychology.

As far as André was concerned (I knew him very well, both before and after his treatment), I can truthfully say, without much fear of error, that his supposed vocation to the priesthood was primarily a neurotic retreat from the responsibilities and risks of living. There was nothing positive in the attraction of the priesthood; in speaking of his future life as a priest, he always referred to its more glamorous aspects. Supposing that he had continued his studies and been ordained, I do not really think that the Church would have been particularly happy at the prospect of one more neurotic priest. There are too many of them already, and they unconsciously pass on their own anxieties and insecurities to the souls who come to them for help: they only serve to increase the confusion between religion and neurosis.

Not that the faith of a neurotic is always and necessarily inauthentic, or that it necessarily disappears with his eventual cure. A person can even have a very serious neurosis and still have a very pure faith. This faith then has no intrinsic relation with the psychic illness and is never threatened by the cure.

Such was the case of a young man named James. Suffering from agoraphobia and a serious neurotic sense of insecurity, he was treated by a famous Freudian psychoanalyst. The results of the treatment were excellent. James' sex life took on a normal orientation, his insecurity and phobias all disappeared. But the psychoanalyst could not yet bring himself to consider the analysis as complete. James' religious fervor, instead of growing less intense, actually increased as the cure progressed.

And the good doctor, an orthodox disciple of Freud, took it as a matter of dogma that no psychically healthy person could be religious.

If spiritual directors had an appropriate foundation in the field of depth psychology, it would not be so difficult for them to tell real theological faith from its neurotic counterparts. A good many misunderstandings, with far-reaching consequences, would thus be avoided, particularly since such priests would be capable of distinguishing between true and false religious vocation.


*III. Still, faith is a protection . . .*

Real theological faith has nothing to fear from psychotherapy or psychoanalysis. But neither is it an infallible remedy for every psychic disorder. It can exist in sick souls as well as healthy souls, in neurotics as well as balanced minds, for the one basic reason that, of its very essence, it is not within the province of psychology.

But it is also true that, in addition to its objective, ontological reality, religious faith always has a subjective aspect as well, and this element *is* within the province of psychology. It is under this aspect that psychotherapy and mental hygiene must be interested in religion.

In stating that there could not possibly be any (authentic) existence without some transcendence, the philosopher Karl Jaspers is obviously speaking on a metaphysical plane. But this is every bit as true from the point of view of psychology. It is precisely because so many peoples' lives are not oriented towards anything that deserves to be called transcendent, that so many souls are suffocating. Such people are always bending back on themselves, and some schizoid condition, if not full schizophrenia, is a constant threat.

Together with Carl Jung, many psychologists have experienced the fact that neurosis is proportionately less widespread in dynamically religious circles than among agnostics. In the light of his very long and rich experience, Jung makes the statement that "of all the neurotic patients who have reached middle age, that is, who are more than 35 years old, there is not a single one whose most fundamental problem was not posed by his religious attitude. Every single one of these patients was sick, in the last analysis, because he had lost the things that a living religious faith has always given to its followers, and no single one of them was ever really cured unless he was able to recover, at the same time, a religious attitude in keeping with what he had lost." *

It goes without saying that Jung and the other psychologists who recognize the immense importance of religious faith in the soul are not speaking from a theological point of view. They are not pronouncing upon the objective truth of the dogmas held by one or another religion. Their only concern is the subjective and psychological conformity between a person's religious attitude and the object of faith.

### IV. Equilibrium and the Moral Self

For a long time, psychologists of the Freudian school, looked upon morality primarily, if not solely, as an arbitrary constraint of the social superego, neurosis being defined as the result of

---

* Jung, *Psychological Healing* . . . . p. 282 (French edition)

conflict between the life instincts of the individual and the moral law. And it went without saying that the personal instincts were always right and the moral law was always wrong. Quite logically, psychic health would then call for an emancipation of the individual's impulses and instincts from their submission to the moral law.

Today, a depth psychologist could hardly escape such an over-simplified view of psychic conflict. * The moral law is not imposed on the individual simply by the social superego. Just as frequently it emanates from the ideal self-image, without which a man could have either spiritual progress nor even real psychic equilibrium. What is more, experience teaches us that many psychic problems are directly caused by the disorder which results from refusing to recognize a moral law. Even supposing, with the Marxists for example, that there is no such thing as an eternal moral law, universally valid, the individual will not be free from the anarchy and slavery of his contrary instincts unless he gives precisely the same submission to the moral code of his time and environment as he would to an eternal code of morality. Even the communists understand this point: they have built a universal morality, in theory at least, on what should have been only the morality of one single class.

Obviously a doctor could claim to cure the problems arising from a conflict between instinct and morality by persuading his patient that there is no moral law objectively good in itself, and that he must not feel guilty when his behavior involves a breach of morality. But, even apart from the many dangers presented by such a sense of morality for the whole of human society, we know that only very few people are able to find any sense of order or direction in a life that is built upon this absolute freedom exalted by such philosophers as Jean-Paul

---

* Cf. *The Depths of the Soul,* ch. VII

Sartre. Nietzsche himself thought only his "supreme" capable of such an effort, and he had to admit, to his own embarrassment, that he himself was not such a "superman."

For the majority of mankind, that is, apart from those who are destined to become "supermen," mental health is possible only through a generous acceptance of the fundamental demands of the moral law. But such acceptance is possible, in practice, only within a religious framework. Only religion has the power to make the inevitable constraints of morality bearable, and even elevating, by making them interior. When he is convinced that he is acting out of love of God, the religious man no longer looks upon the moral law as an outstanding power curtailing the freedom of his existence. None of the disorders which Freud attributes to the superego can seriously threaten such a person. Provided of course that his religion is really theological.

It would be a mistake to compare sacramental confession, such as it is practiced in the Catholic Church for example, with the other type of confession which plays such an important role in modern psychotherapy. The first is concerned only with those sins of which the conscious mind knows itself to be guilty, whereas the second penetrates deep into the secrets of the unconscious mind which is, by definition, beyond responsibility and hence not subject to sins as such. This is not to deny the fact that the peace of soul which results from mental confession greatly promotes the dissolution of the unconscious sense of guilt. To know that God has pardoned him helps a man become free of all his doubts and anxieties.

On the other hand it would be pointless to look to the confessional for the exclusive cure of a scrupulous person. Neurosis is already well established in such a case, and only after the dissolution of his unconscious sense of guilt (by the techniques proper to psychotherapy) can confession and absolution hope to contribute anything to restoring his real peace of soul.

*V. The Ideal Self.*

We insisted, in chapter II, on the primary importance of a lofty set of ideals for the normal and harmonious psychic development of the child. Parents first of all, and then friends and teachers, must be a prolonged incarnation of the perfection towards which the child aspires in a confused way at first. A lofty set of ideals helps the young person break the spell of narcissism and turn towards the outside world; it gives him the indispensable desire to grow up.

Unfortunately, parents, friends and teachers are very seldom so perfect as the young person likes to imagine. It is thus inevitable that this admiration will eventually give way to disillusion. Every psychologist has treated many patients whose neurosis dates back essentially to the time when the ideal images of their childhood first started to tumble.

There is only one ideal of self that never fails: God. Certain parents, narcissistically attached to their children, are making a very big mistake when they object to the fact that in catechism instruction their sons and daughters are taught to love God or Christ even "more than Mommy and Daddy." It is only by loving God above all else that they have a good chance of always loving the parents as well. It is also very important for their idea of God to be close to the reality and truth as humanly possible. If there is too much talk of fearing God as a policeman who guarantees and upholds a certain social order, then when the individual, on some future day, has — or thinks he has — a good reason for going counter to that particular social order, his faith in God, and thus his whole system of inner security, will be completely and irreparably ruined.

Psychotherapy frequently finds itself in an embarrassing position. The doctor has succeeded in freeing the patient of his neurosis but he realizes that this is not enough. The emotional energy previously mobilized by the neurotic conflict is now free to play a primary role in the patient's existence. Professional interests, or genuine love, can sometimes fill this need. But what about the person who has no professional activity and can find no real interest in his work? What about the woman whose recently cured neurosis has been caused precisely by the fact that she has been disappointed in love? Psychotherapy has cured her neurosis, but the object of her love is still just as far beyond her grasp as before. Where is the avenue that leads to an adequate expression of the libido that has just been freed from neurosis?

It is not within the province of the psychologist to preach renunciation and self-sacrifice. But there is some renunciation and suffering that is, humanly speaking, unavoidable, and only the practice of accepting them in the spirit of religion can make them not only bearable, but even elevating. Only faith can orient the undirected libido towards charitable activities which can at least partially overcome the feeling of frustration.

The knowledge that they are children of God, brothers of Christ, members of the communion of saints — this can give courage and confidence to even the most unfortunate and tormented souls, even to those who no longer have anything to hope for on the plane of natural existence. In a living faith they will be able to find a workable defense against the feelings of insecurity which plague them. Meditation on the mysteries of the Incarnation and redemption is a school that plunges us deep into an immense ocean of divine life. No matter how little favored we are in the gifts and graces of nature, even if there is no single human being to love us, faith assures us that God loves us just as much as he loves those who are crowned with every earthly blessing, that we are not condemned to live as mere cogs in a vast and meaningless impersonal machinery. Eucharistic Communion, in a spirit of faith, is particularly well equipped to fill the soul with this comforting sense of friendship with the Absolute.

Whatever the personal religious convictions of the psychologist, he cannot help but admit the fact that faith is, actually, the most powerful factor in the promotion of human existence. Obviously, too, for that faith to promote a maximum of mental health, there must be some religious training in the family and in a church — a definite break with the rationalistic prejudices left over from the nineteenth century. It is not the so-called logical "proofs" for the existence of God that have the power to shelter human souls from the many perils lurking within their unconscious mind. Psychologically speaking, only a living faith, that is, a faith which embraces a man's whole emotional orientation, can hope to achieve such an essential objective.

# 8 professional help

## 1. *The "Ordinary Ministers" of Mental Hygiene*

Normally speaking, the application of the advice and precepts of mental hygiene does not require the services of a specialist. Just like bodily hygiene, it must enter into our everyday habit: it is a matter for individual application.

As far as the young child is concerned, it will obviously be the parents who first teach him how to take effective precautions against the threat of psychic harm. In due time, the professional educators will add their efforts to those of the parents: kindergarten teachers, teachers, professors .... In some cases, they might even be called upon to make up for what is missing in the family. But this they can do only if the harm done by the negligence or ignorance of the parents has not been too serious.

Many children look to a kindergarten teacher or a nurse for the understanding and affection and sense of security which their own mothers could not give them — because they were too ignorant or too involved in their own neurotic conflicts. For others, it will be a priest, or a catechist, a confessor or a spiritual director who can give them (particularly in the case of little boys) what they could not get from their mothers. The custom, which is a general one in most parts of the world, of calling every priest "Father," makes it much easier for the priest or minister to accomplish this supplementary role.

In order for teachers, priests, and religious brothers and nuns, to be successful in their mission of completing or supplying the mental hygiene the child needs to have, they should have a rather solid grounding in the elementary principles of psychology. Without such an initiation, they might very well make mistakes whose repercussions would generally be much more serious than those resulting from the behavior of awkward or ignorant parents. A few elementary notions about psychology are generally enough for parents who are not laboring under the influence of an overly rigid superego, to enable them to keep their children from the most obvious psychic problems and help them resolve their conflicts in a positive way. Instinct, with a minimum of scientific procedure, is an almost infallible guide in this area.

But the professional educator, lacking all biological bonds with the child, cannot count on instinct. He might have intuition however, and this can be a most effective tool in establishing proper relationship with the children he instructs. But a teacher can pride himself in his intuition only if it goes hand in hand with solid scientific knowledge.

In normal teachers' colleges, just as well as in seminaries and novitiates for religious who will pursue a teaching vocation, the instruction in depth psychology, psycho-pedagogy, and psychological hygiene, should be given much more serious attention than now appears to be the case. Future professors of secondary education also need to be convinced that the human sciences mentioned above are much more important to the proper exercise of their profession than the painstaking preparation for their comprehensives — so often more a work for memory than intelligence — which is currently the substance of their accreditation.

## II. The Specialist's Role

There are some cases in which neither the parents nor the educators are in a position to act effectively. The farther the germs of neurosis have already penetrated into the child's psyche, the more necessary it is to correct the mistake made by parents and educators. The specialist whose services are then indispensable is the child psychologist.

In almost every case, parents do not decide to consult a psychologist until their child begins to show serious signs of neurosis. The treatment is then, of necessity, a rather long one, notwithstanding the immense progress realized in this field since the time of Freud, and it does not always produce the desired results. On the other hand, there is a good chance that, if the specialist is consulted from the very first signs of psychic disorder, the psychic conflict can find an adequate expression without degenerating into neurosis. This goes not only for children, but also for adults.

Mrs. F. consulted a psychotherapist because, after ten years of marriage, her husband had just taken a mistress and was threatening to abandon her. In this new woman he had discovered that warm depth of love that he could never find in his own wife, whose basic frigidity had been obvious from the outset. At the beginning of their marriage, it would have been no great problem for an experienced psychiatrist to help resolve the obstacles that prevented the full development of the young bride's love life, and thereby considerably increase her chances for a successful marriage.

As it is now, the psychotherapist still does have a chance to succeed in solving the problem of frigidity, but there is little hope that the harmony of the young couple can ever be restored. It is always a thousand times easier to avoid the breaking than it is to pick up the pieces.

Anthony had shown unequivocal signs of psychic imbalance from the age of five. His sad moods and his happy moods were both equally excessive, violently out of proportion to their real causes. A very timid and backward child, he adapted poorly to the society of other children. He felt secure only with his mother: his own father terrified him.

Anthony's parents were not too familiar with current psychological problems: it never occurred to them that they should consult a doctor. Instead, they paid as little attention as possible to their son's problems, convinced that things would take care of themselves, "in due time." As it actually turned out, time changed nothing. At the age of puberty, Anthony's troubles assumed such an obviously pathological character that it was no longer enough to ask the advice of a good psychologist; a long and expensive clinical treatment was the only answer.

### III. When to Visit the Doctor.

It would be wrong to be too severe on those who do not consult a psychiatrist early enough, either for their own troubles or those of their children. Such problems can arise in any person, and with great frequency: most of the time the popular methods of psychological hygiene are enough to meet the crisis, provided the measures are applied at once. Thus it is difficult, if not impossible, to set up a rule that is universally valid for cases in which a doctor should be consulted.

As far as children are concerned, a good deal depends on how conversant their parents are with psychology and mental health. Enlightened and reasonably well balanced parents can apply the prescriptions of mental hygiene by themselves, as long as their child does not give evidence of any characteristic anomaly. On the other hand, as soon as character or behavior problems of some seriousness begin to show up, as soon as there is some danger of serious deviation in the emotional maturity of the child, then it is good to consult a specialist, if only to reassure themselves.

The vast majority of psychic problems that beset the child do not need real psychotherapy. An experienced psychologist will quickly notice how the general principles of mental hygiene should be adapted to a given child in given circumstances. Most of the time, the problems can be straightened out if the parents and other persons who have daily contact with the disturbed child will change their attitude towards him.

Chantal was a litle girl of seven, intelligent and charming. There was only one thing that concerned her mother: she obstinately refused to "grow up." She continued to act like a baby in many respects. For example, she would sleep only in her mother's bed and she demanded many of the attentions a mother gives only to a baby. Her mother finally realized how dangerous this could be for her child's future development. She tried to send the girl on outings, or to a summer camp. But without success: Chantal stubbornly refused to be separated from her mother. The psychologist, in his discussions with the little girl, discovered that she had a great admiration for a little girl of her own age who was very "emancipated" and well balanced. He advised the mother to have Chantal's little friend invite her to the summer camp. Chantal was delighted to accept the invitation and looked forward to the experience. At first, she was homesick for her mother. But since she had wanted the separation herself, it no longer looked like something frightening or like a punishment. Little by little she adapted to the group life of the camp. Her behavior towards her mother took on a more detached note and her whole psychic growth was quite normal. But without the doctor's judicious advice, it is very likely that the little girl would have formed a fixation on her infantile dependence upon her mother — and this, in turn, would almost surely have led to some neurotic involvement when she grew to adulthood.

Adults themselves need no other outside help in order to

effectively observe the rules of psychological hygiene such as we have explained them in this volume. These are very simple matters, and can become habits as spontaneous as brushing your teeth every day.

The man who is well grounded in depth psychology and thus in a position to see to his own mental hygiene, can do very much, by himself, to neutralize the effects of latent neurosis. But all it takes is a change of some magnitude in his situation — marriage, the birth of a child, change of profession — and he will falter: he will be unable to face his altered situation. The advice of a good doctor can be a great advantage in such circumstances.

In the domain of mental hygiene, the first and principal duty of the psychologist is to educate parents, educators, advisers, spiritual directors, and heads of religious orders. Even when mental hygiene is not equal to the task of preventing neurosis, it can always take the form of therapy.